How To Play
Your Best
Tennis
All the
Time

Jack Kramer

with **Larry Sheehan**

How to Play Your Best Tennis All the Time

illustrated by Ray Caram

ATHENEUM / SMI   NEW YORK   1977

Portions of Part V originally appeared in the May and June 1977 issues of Tennis, The Magazine of Racquet Sports.

LIBRARY OF CONGRESS CATALOGING IN PUBLICATION DATA

Kramer, Jack.
   How to play your best tennis all the time.

   1. Tennis.   I. Sheehan, Larry, joint author.
II. Title.
GV995.K69   1977   791.34'22   76-53402
ISBN 0-689-10757-9

COPYRIGHT © 1977 BY JACK KRAMER AND LARRY SHEEHAN
ALL RIGHTS RESERVED
PUBLISHED SIMULTANEOUSLY IN CANADA BY
MCCLELLAND AND STEWART LTD.
COMPOSITION BY DIX TYPESETTING CO., INC.,
SYRACUSE, NEW YORK
PRINTED AND BOUND BY THE MURRAY PRINTING CO.,
FORGE VILLAGE, MASSACHUSETTS
DESIGNED BY KATHLEEN CAREY
FIRST EDITION

Contents

Part I Preliminaries

Why Everyone Should Play to Win

My longtime friend and physician Dr. Omar Fareed has a tennis court behind his offices not far from where I live in Los Angeles, and he's been running a kind of Average Man's Wimbledon there every day for years.

Omar has a lot of pals among the mad-for-tennis folks in the entertainment industry out here. Plus, anyone who becomes one of Omar's patients eventually is converted to tennis even if he's never seen a racket before, because the good doctor believes firmly in tennis's role as a healer and rejuvenator.

Anyway, Omar has a huge pool of players to draw on to keep his court hopping.

These men play a friendly but ferocious, no-holds-barred brand of tennis, I've noticed. If you have a weakness in your game, they'll hammer at it. If you're out of shape, they'll run you down. When I played doubles over there for fun on a regular basis some years ago, after retiring from the pro game, I had an ailing hip that greatly reduced my mobility. It wasn't long before they found it out. All I saw after that were deep lobs.

I mention Omar's tennis-playing friends here at the outset for two reasons.

First, I think their competitive zeal brings out the game's recreational benefits to the fullest. These players try hard to win, without being bad sports about it, or letting it ruin their day if they don't win. And by putting everything they have on the line during matches, they not only test themselves to their natural limits, they also bring out the best in their opponents. You can play a sport like golf solely for the exercise, if you like, and limit no one's potential but your own. In tennis you may be undermining the value of the game for everyone unless you really do try to win.

Second, watching Omar's players over the years has been an invaluable aid to me in figuring out the major problems people have in learning to play tennis effectively. The problems I've tried to help these players with are representative of the problems faced by the vast majority of recreational tennis players. In a nutshell, these problems are:

3

- Faulty grips.
- Mechanical failures in stroke production.
- Playing in a style unsuited to one's physique, emotional makeup, or shotmaking repertory, out of vanity or ignorance.
- Playing too good a shot from a deep position.
- Overhitting.
- Playing the wrong shot on crucial points.
- Inventing shots instead of playing tried-and-true shots.
- Not lobbing enough.
- Failing to evaluate opponents correctly.

The approach presented in this book is designed to help players avoid or minimize these problems. It is presented in three stages: Stage One is devoted to building the basic ground game:

- Understanding the basic concepts of ball spin and racket control.
- Practicing groundstrokes to groove a powerful overspin-producing forehand and a controlled underspin-producing backhand.
- Building a consistent slice serve.
- Learning to play shots off the bounce according to the height and speed of the ball and your position in the court.

Stage Two is devoted to finding your own point-winning combinations:

- Analyzing your physical and emotional makeup to determine the playing style best suited for you, whether it be one of attack, of counterattack, or of a steady baseline game.
- Playing a lot of doubles to become familiar with the major auxiliary shots in tennis—the lob, volley, and overhead.
- Learning the approach shot theory and basic volley tactics.

Stage Three is about competing:

- Analyzing opponents.
- Learning the art of match preparation and play.

Naturally, this approach reflects my own experience in learning the game, from my first teacher, Dick Skeen, and from probably the single biggest influence in my development, Cliff Roche. It was "Coach" Roche, an engineer by profession and a brilliant one, who taught me to analyze tennis in terms of the true percentage shots and tactics in the game.

It also draws upon my experience as a player—winning Wimbledon, Forest Hills, and Davis Cup as an amateur, and then turning pro and winning arduous challenge-match tours over Bobby Riggs, Pancho Segura, Frank Sedgman, and Pancho Gonzales.

My approach adheres closely to fundamentals in strokemaking and to a sound tactical application of all your shots. I think it will have relevance for any young would-be Wimbledon champ. But it is the ordinary players—such as grace Omar's court day in and day out—who are foremost in my thoughts.

This is as it should be, for it is the ordinary players who are the real stars in the present tennis boom.

The Special Challenge of Tennis

If I had to describe tennis to a visitor from another planet, who was curious about our games and sports, I suppose I would make the following points.

Tennis is a game that asks for quick bursts of energy and fast reactions with arms and legs. It deserves more credit than it usually gets as a tough physical activity—it's really in a league with such sports as boxing, basketball, and water polo. It favors the fit player, and wears down and frustrates the player who is out of shape or overweight and so can't cover his or her side of the court.

Tennis is too difficult a game for anyone to play flawlessly. That is why errors decide who wins a match, not great winning shots. Everyone has weaknesses and they do not vanish just because it's Sunday and you're in a match with somebody you would particularly like to beat. Perfectionists get no gratification when they play the game. Even good players have some strokes that work and some that don't, and only three or four spots on the court that they can consistently hit for winners or forcing shots. The dominant players on the pro circuit are dethroned at frequent intervals because even these superb athletic specimens can't play the game right all the time.

Tennis demands a knack or instinct for evaluating your true potential in hitting or retrieving balls. Accurate self-analysis is often what separates the winners from the also-rans in the game, regardless of physical skills. It is not to be confused with raw IQ—you don't have to be a Rhodes Scholar to succeed in tennis. But you must be able to identify and develop your particular playing strengths and have the patience to mold them into one or more point-winning combinations that you can use during matches.

That said, I should quickly add that tennis is a game that, once begun, is played more effectively with a minimum of cerebral activity. Good players get more credit for thinking on the court than they deserve. When they're competing effectively they're on automatic pilot out there, doing what they do best, and doing it over and over again. They don't think unless absolutely forced to.

Tennis doesn't give luck much of a role in the outcome of matches. If your "equipment"—your shotmaking ability and your winning combinations—give you an edge on another player, you will win eight or nine times out of ten, unless you're overconfident, sick, or your racket breaks. That's why there are so many lopsided rivalries in the game.

Under the traditional deuce scoring system, in which a player must win a game by at least two points, luck is further minimized, for the margin of victory required helps the better player to keep control, and gives only fleeting pleasure to the specialist in off-the-wood shots, bad bounces, and other "oncers."

Tennis has a highly unpredictable time framework. Unlike most sports, in tennis you're not quite sure who's going to win until you're absolutely sure, which is after the last point is played. It takes as much emotional stamina and concentration to retain a lead as it does to come from behind. The suspense can be a strain on the player of questionable nerve or self-confidence. If you can become the better player from love–5 in games and love–40 in that sixth game, you'll win the set.

6

Also unlike most sports, tennis depends on a shared respect for fair play in order for the game to be played at all. In many other games, the idea tends to be to get away with everything you can, if the umpire or the ref isn't looking—rather like the tack otherwise good citizens like to take in filing their income tax. Anyway, in tennis you can't do anything deliberately to disturb your opponent's ability to play, and whenever you're in doubt about a line call, you must make the decision in favor of the opponent. That way you'll feel better about yourself—and you won't run out of people to play with.

I think it's important to be aware of these various subjective factors because, taken together, they are what make tennis unique, so tremendously challenging, and, more than any other single sport, universal in its appeal. Don't lose sight of them and you'll accept much more readily the early difficulties in learning the mechanics of good strokemaking, and the inevitable disappointments in playing your first actual matches.

ADVICE TO PARENTS

I used to think there was no need to hurry in introducing kids to tennis. In fact I thought they were better off not starting until they were ten, eleven, or twelve. In the meantime they could participate in sports like baseball, softball, basketball, football, soccer, and field hockey. There, I reasoned, they would get the general idea of sports and also begin to develop the coordination and footwork that would benefit them later on the tennis court. The skipping motion you might use in guarding a player in basketball, for instance, translates readily into the kind of footwork you need in tennis.

So I used to think that letting the kids take part in all these various team sports first was fine and proper. Now I feel differently. I think you should expose your child to tennis at about the time he or she is exposed to the various team sports—which is about eight years old. Why? Because if you don't, there is a very good chance that Little League baseball, or some other highly organized activity, is going to hook them!

At such an early age, of course, no child can be expected to pay

7

attention for long periods of time, or to handle even a minisized racket with a great deal of skill. So it is vital that whoever introduces tennis to a child possess tremendous *patience,* and that the principal aim of the activity remain *fun.*

No formal lessons should be given to children except in a group. There are two advantages to group lessons, especially at the beginning.

1. You learn more in a group because you have the benefit of seeing other people make mistakes and hearing these mistakes corrected repeatedly by the instructor. You're hearing and watching and it rubs off on you. Often you can learn more from somebody else's mistake than from your own—especially if you're the self-conscious type.

2. Solo lessons tend to bring out the impulse to show off or please in pupils, rather than a more fundamental drive to improve. When you are in a group, you are competing—trying to equal or excel your fellow students—consciously or not.

About Ball Spin

Baseball rewards fair balls hit out of the playing area, so sluggers like Ted Williams or Hank Aaron never really had to worry about control over the balls they hit. But tennis penalizes shots that don't land inside the baseline and the sidelines. The secret to keeping shots within bounds in tennis is controlling the spin on the ball. So before we get into the actual mechanics of stroke execution, let's look at spin briefly.

The flight of a tennis ball is controlled through a combination of gravity and spin. Gravity alone won't keep a ball in play. A serve hit firmly but without spin would not only miss the service box—it would go beyond the baseline. A groundstroke hit with any firmness would also go beyond the dimensions of the 27-by-78-foot single court, before gravity brought it down to earth. A shot hit softly at an angle would still go outside the sidelines. A shot hit softly all the way from one baseline to the other baseline just might stay in—but it wouldn't pose much of a problem for the other player.

In other words, spin must be imparted to the ball in some degree. A brushing or biting action of the racket strings during the interval of impact accomplishes this. I use the word "interval" to promote the idea of a prolonged period of contact between racket strings and ball, and not an instantaneous hit or slap.

Actually, Vic Braden—one of the game's most innovative teachers, and one of our most tenacious researchers in the technique of tennis—has taken high-speed photographs that reveal the racket strings hit the ball *twice* on every stroke. At the instant of contact the ball rebounds off the strings. Then the strings catch up with the ball and hit it again. While this may indicate a need to reword the "double-hit" rule in tennis (you're not supposed to hit the ball twice), it is too finite as a physical phenomenon for our human senses to grasp usefully. I think it's important simply to imagine that the racket strings act upon the ball as a stiff bristle brush might. It is by "brushing" the ball for as long as possible that you are able to impart the degree of spin you need, for absolute control. Brush *up* on the ball with the racket strings—as you do when the path of the racket on the forward swing goes from a low to a high position—and you will produce topspin, or overspin. When a ball has topspin, it rotates rapidly end over end in the direction that the ball is moving. The shot flies in a half-moon trajectory over the net and drops sharply on the other side.

Brush *down* on the ball, and you will produce a shot with backspin, or underspin. When a ball rotates end over end in the opposite direction it is traveling, the shot clears the net more slowly and by a greater margin, and it drops more rapidly once it has reached its peak.

In these two examples, I have made the assumption that the racket face itself is just about square during impact. By that I mean, the frame of the racket is perpendicular to the ground. So it is the path of the racket that creates the exact brushing action. But topspin or underspin can also be imparted by "closing" or "opening" the racket face during the interval of impact. That means tilting

9

ALL TENNIS SHOTS
MUST CARRY SPIN

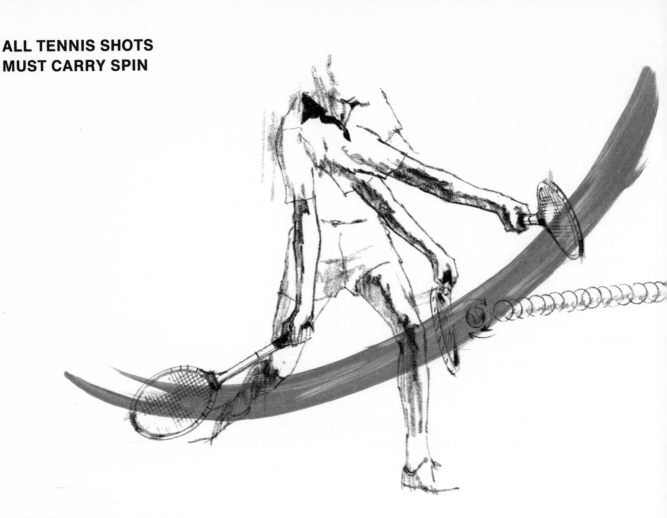

FIGURE 1

the frame of the racket toward the net or toward the back fence, as you stroke. On short strokes such as the volley or the lob, where underspin is desirable for control, or height is needed for defense, that's what happens.

10   The important thing to note for now is that the brushing action,

development of strokes which impart enough rota-
to the ball is the key to control and consistency in
nis. In fact no shot can be hit with reasonable firm-
s without some kind of spin on it. If the shot were
perfectly flat—with the racket head held perpen-
lar to the surface throughout the interval of im-
t—the ball would go outside the lines or carry
ittle speed that the opposing player could re-
it effortlessly.

is easier to understand the interaction of
nis racket and ball if you imagine a stiff,
tle-type brush in place of the racket
gs. Topspin is produced when the

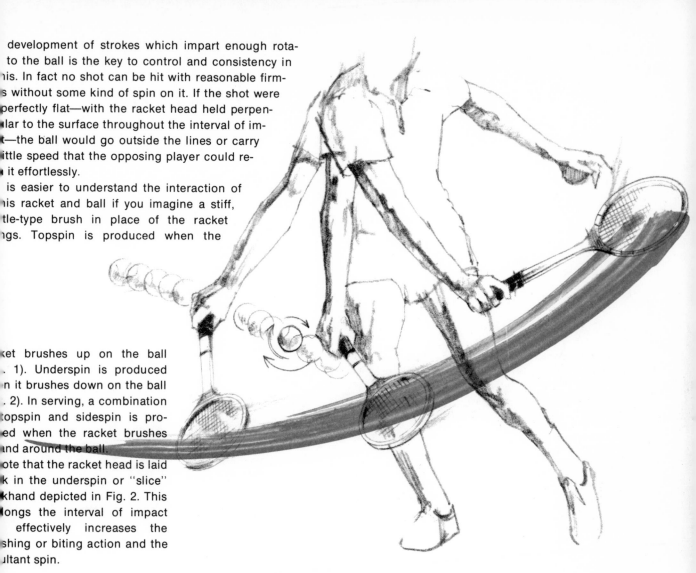

ket brushes up on the ball
. 1). Underspin is produced
n it brushes down on the ball
. 2). In serving, a combination
topspin and sidespin is pro-
ed when the racket brushes
and around the ball.
ote that the racket head is laid
k in the underspin or "slice"
khand depicted in Fig. 2. This
longs the interval of impact
effectively increases the
shing or biting action and the
ultant spin.

FIGURE 2

created by the path the racket face takes during the forward swing,
or the alignment of the racket face at impact, or a combination
of both, brings the two-ounce tennis ball under control. With spin,
you can hit balls much harder and still keep them in the court.
That's what we're after in groundstrokes and on the serve. 11

Part II Fundamentals of Groundstrokes

Ball Control from the Baseline

Why do you suppose Ken Rosewall could reach the final at both Wimbledon and Forest Hills in his fortieth year? Why are Pancho Gonzales, Rod Laver, and Roy Emerson so tough to beat even though they're also well past their playing prime? Why is Pancho Segura in his middle fifties such a threat on the burgeoning pro senior circuit against players ten years his junior?

The answer is that, though the stamina and power of youth may be gone from their careers, these players possess a *defensive* game that is as sound as it was back when they were winning most of the matches they played.

The defensive game is based primarily on control of the ball on serves and on groundstrokes. It requires knowledge of how to produce spin on shots through the action of your racket in the stroke, and a sensible "percentage" application of the shots available to you. It is the key to developing the steadiness and consistency on the court that causes an opponent to make errors and give you points. It is indisputably the only logical style of playing tennis for the majority of weekend players, and it has the added advantage of being a style that does not really wear with age, or rust too much from neglect. It is effective at every level of play, from novice to pro.

Coming from Jack Kramer, this emphasis on defensive baseline play, with a high priority given to forehands and backhands, may sound surprising. You may have heard of my reputation as "the man who institutionalized the Big Game in tennis," or as "the serve-and-volley player par excellence."

Actually I learned a steady defensive style of play first, and I've never regretted it.

I was eleven when I took up tennis. In those days—in the 1930s —the big names in the game were Bill Tilden, the Englishman Fred Perry, Ellsworth Vines, Don Budge, and Bobby Riggs. Budge and Riggs, only a few years my senior, were the young lions of the tennis world as I started competing.

With the possible exception of Vines, who generated such phenomenal power on his serve that it was only natural for him to lean on that stroke through many a match, all the leading players

15

of the age overcame their opponents by controlling the ball with shots played *from the backcourt.* They concentrated on returning serve adeptly, so the opponent could not safely come in following serve. They seldom attacked immediately behind their own serve. They hit solid, well-placed forehands and backhands until they forced a weak, short ball, and then they did attack, moving to net behind the approach shot to complete the kill with winning volleys.

These were the players on whom I modeled my own game. As a result I grooved a solid forehand and a dependable if not spectacular underspin backhand, long before I paid much attention to volleying at all.

There was another good reason to specialize in groundstrokes before all else in those days. Most major junior competition of the time was held on slow surfaces where duels from the backcourt were inevitable.

Only later, when I began to compete on the fast grass surfaces on which the big men's titles were contested in those days—Wimbledon, Forest Hills, Longwood, and the various Davis Cup sites—did the extra-strong serve that had evolved in my game begin to give me a decided advantage. To exploit the weak returns that were made off my fast, skidding, wide serves on grass, I hustled in to intercept the opponent's return in the air and volley it away. I wasn't afraid to be lobbed, if my first volley had not scored an outright winner, because, along with my serve, I also possessed a naturally strong and dependable overhead smash. I could cover all but the most skillfully played lobs and put them away for the point.

This sequence of serve, volley, overhead was the winning combination in my game that gained the most publicity.

Without the groundstroke capability, however, I would not have been able to keep the proper amount of pressure on my opponents when I was returning their serves, and on slow surfaces my power game often would have been nullified by their passing shots. When circumstances dictated, I was able to give up the net game and only come in on short balls—just as Tilden and the others had done.

Though this trend seems to have been reversed, for a time many youngsters in this country wanted nothing else but to become whiz-

CTICAL ADVANTAGES OF TOPSPIN

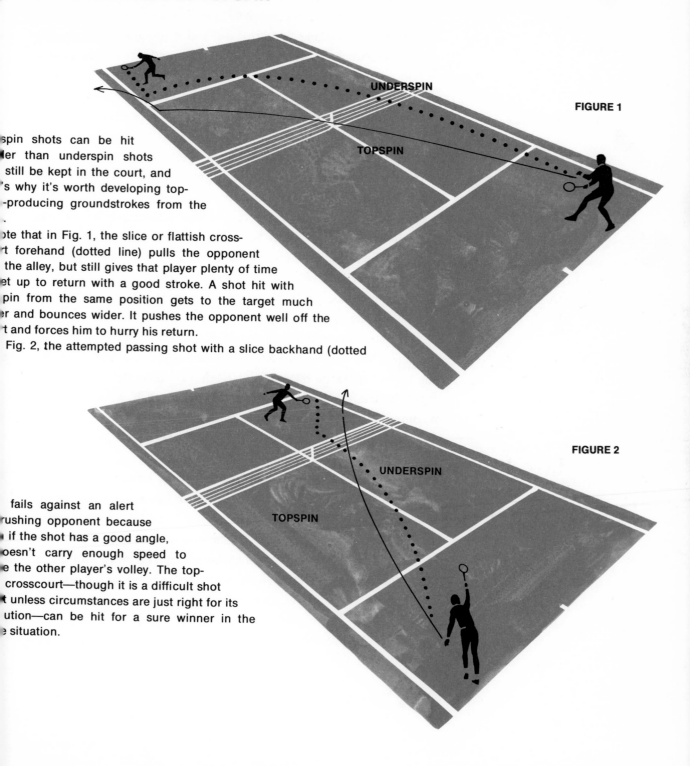

UNDERSPIN

TOPSPIN

FIGURE 1

UNDERSPIN

TOPSPIN

FIGURE 2

spin shots can be hit
er than underspin shots
still be kept in the court, and
's why it's worth developing top-
-producing groundstrokes from the

te that in Fig. 1, the slice or flattish cross-
t forehand (dotted line) pulls the opponent
the alley, but still gives that player plenty of time
et up to return with a good stroke. A shot hit with
pin from the same position gets to the target much
r and bounces wider. It pushes the opponent well off the
t and forces him to hurry his return.
Fig. 2, the attempted passing shot with a slice backhand (dotted

fails against an alert
rushing opponent because
if the shot has a good angle,
oesn't carry enough speed to
e the other player's volley. The top-
crosscourt—though it is a difficult shot
t unless circumstances are just right for its
ution—can be hit for a sure winner in the
situation.

bang serve-and-volley players. Many of them thought they were copying my power game, or that of Pancho Gonzales, the big server who came along just after me and made a tremendous impact. Interestingly, Pancho did gain his big amateur victories largely on the strength of his serve, but his game didn't become truly complete until he was forced to improve his groundstrokes after losing to me on tour, 27 matches to 96. I had been forced to give up *my* big serve in order to beat Bobby Riggs in a previous head-to-head tour—you learn a lot when you turn pro!

In any event, an awful lot of boys growing up in the 1950s and 1960s—encouraged by a fair number of coaches and teachers who perhaps should have known better—learned to attack before they knew how to defend. Many never did learn solid baseline tactics, and ended with incomplete, highly vulnerable tennis games.

As my experience with Riggs on our tour made me realize, there's nothing aggressive about hitting a big serve if your opponent can block it back past you every time.

Too many young players have equated "defensive" with "weak" or "tentative." There was certainly never anything tentative about the way Don Budge returned serve. He may have remained at the baseline, but he hit *bullets* back at you. And as we shall see, I recommend that beginners start hitting with topspin—the faster and more potentially aggressive ball spin—on both forehands and backhands.

Anyway, the trend toward over-emphasizing serve and volley has been stopped at last. Jimmy Connors and Bjorn Borg are among numerous rising young stars in the game today who have demonstrated magnificent control from the baseline. For youngsters beginning in tennis now, these stars have helped restore prestige to the groundstrokes. That is how it should be, and where we will begin. . . .

Once you realize how effective and durable a solid ground game can be, you'll be willing to put in the time and effort required to groove and standardize the basic strokes.

I'm a firm believer in practice, repetition and hitting as many balls as possible in exactly the same way, on the theory that the more you do something, the better you get at it. It's a no-frills plan, basically, and it helps to build consistency and breed confidence.

Later, when you begin playing matches, there won't be time to worry about details of execution. If you treated each ball hit to you during a match as a brand-new problem to be solved, you would become confused. In actual play you've got to forget about technique and concentrate on tactics. You've got to think *where* you want to hit it, and not *how* to hit it. If you're groping for your grip or conscious of trying to get the racket back early, then you haven't practiced enough. Mechanical weaknesses lose more points than mental lapses. Good players are on automatic pilot out there.

In the following pages I outline this approach to developing your groundstrokes:

* Acquire a good ready position and the proper grips.
* Learn to run, bend your knees and use footwork so that you can meet the ball on all groundstrokes at about the same height and distance from your body.
* Practice a smooth transfer of weight on all shots, to generate power—pace on the ball—without undue effort.
* Swing the racket in the same fluid motion from both sides— from a low position to a high position so that you brush up on the ball with the strings and produce topspin.
* Understand the minor difference between forehands and backhands which occur on the backswing, forward swing, and finish —so that you do not fail to adhere to the *major* similarities.

Depending on your athletic ability, vigor, and enthusiasm, it may take you anywhere from a month to a year to get this far. But at the end of this process you will emerge with an aggressive forehand stroke and a sound defensive backhand. Combined with a

Building Better Ground- strokes

reasonably dependable serve (treated elsewhere), these strokes will create the foundation for a rock-solid tennis game.

ON PRACTICE There are a few good ways to practice groundstrokes.

The most effective method at the start is to hit against a ball-tossing machine, which will feed you shots that bounce in the same spot in the court at the rate of about 15 balls a minute. In an hour you could hit some 600 balls, with breaks to catch your breath. If you played two sets in one hour, you'd be lucky to hit as many as 200 balls, because there's so much time lost between points.

Hitting against the machine would help you get your basic stroking motion down pat before you took on the challenge of the more varied types of bouncing balls you would face in any real exchange with another player. So you could acquire a good technical stroke and then gradually take on the challenge of footwork and of setting up for balls that come at you from different directions and angles, at varying speeds and in a multitude of bounces.

These machines are increasingly common at tennis clubs and court complexes and often are rented quite inexpensively for use on practice lanes that don't take up a full court.

Groundstrokes may be practiced against a wall, too, provided you avoid falling into the habit of overhitting. If you stand 39 feet from the wall—the distance between baseline and net on an actual court—you would have to really pound the ball against the wall to get it back to you on one bounce. That's bad, because in actual play it's the smooth stroke, not the hard one, that produces effective power. If you use the wall, move in 10 to 15 feet closer—so you can stroke smoothly every time. That means the ball will come back at you awfully fast, but that's okay. It will force you to change your grips and get your racket back more quickly.

When practicing with another player on a full court, underhitting is as much an impediment to developing the proper weight shift on groundstrokes as overhitting is. Many players underhit out of fear of making the ball go too far. Aim to clear the net by at least three or four feet—as though the net were twice its actual height—and don't worry if you clear the baseline by that much as

20

well, in the early stages of grooving your game. Make your mistakes long or wide, and not short or into the net. If you became preoccupied with keeping the ball in the court, you would unconsciously inhibit your weight shift, or eliminate it altogether. Depth on your shots will force more short balls on your opponent's shots. And, as we'll see later on, eliciting short balls is the key to developing successful point-winning combinations for most players.

Also when practicing with another player, make sure both of you avoid politely hitting *to* each other, back and forth down the middle. You should be trying to find out what you can do in moving three or four steps and then hitting the ball, rather than what you can do when the ball is hit right to you, practice-machine style.

All the great tennis players seem to have had at least two things in common— a fine ready position in preparation for shots, and wonderful grips.

The ready position is the physical and mental attitude you assume before and after every groundstroke.

It's also the position you assume waiting to return serve, following your own serve, and—insofar as speed of play makes it feasible —before and after every volley when you're up at net. Make it part and parcel of your practice of forehands and backhands from the start, and it will automatically occur in your setup for these more advanced shotmaking situations later on. Your "position" of readiness in the court may vary, but the position or posture of your body and even your mind in relation to the next stage of the action, should not vary that much at all.

I would describe a good ready position more precisely as follows:

You are standing watchfully but relaxed, facing the net, with knees bent, weight slightly forward but in good balance. Your feet are comfortably set apart, to about the width of your shoulders, with toes pointing slightly outward—like a duck. You're practically in motion—except that you're not in motion. The closest equiva-

Two Constants of Superior Play

lent posture in sport would be that of a guard in basketball just before the ball is thrown in to his man. Your right hand is in the forehand grip, and your left hand holds the racket lightly at the throat.

What are the benefits of a good ready position?

It promotes a rapid and smooth change to the backhand grip, when that is necessary, and as we'll explain in more detail shortly.

It helps you move more readily into position to hit a shot coming to either side. Whether you have to pivot and step just once to take the ball, or skip and scramble all the way over to the sideline to get it, you're out of the starting gate marginally faster when you're poised to go either way.

And the good ready position promotes better general attentiveness to play and so greater anticipation of where, when, and how the ball is coming over the net to your side.

"Keeping your eye on the ball" is an aspect of a good ready position, and instrumental to good timing in strokemaking, but that's not all you "keep" on the ball.

René Lacoste, the great French player of the 1930s, is also a brilliant thinker and innovator in the game, and a few years ago he made me hit with a racket he had designed. It had rubber stops on the frame that muted the sound of the ball against the strings. His ingenious and quite reasonable theory was that if you took away the *sound* of your shots, you would hinder your opponent's power to anticipate. It reminded me of the importance that Helen Hull Jacobs always put on paying attention to all the *audible* aspects in the flight of the ball—the sound of the ball bouncing on her opponent's court, of the ball striking the opponent's racket strings, of the ball bouncing on her side, and finally the sound of it striking her own racket. Jacob's practice habit depended on *hearing* the shots in tennis as well as seeing them—keeping your ear on the ball, to put it plainly. Lacoste's muting device prevents the sense of hearing from being useful as honing equipment for the opponent.

My problem with the device was simply that I liked to hear my *own* shots, as I suspect most good players would. Nevertheless, the Crocodile's strategem impressed on me anew the fact that antici-

LING READY

od ready position in tennis is similar to that of a
r guarding his man in basketball, who is ready
ove to right or left without delay or loss of bal-
. Though it is of particular importance on the
n of serve, it is an attitude of body that players
ld strive to assume immediately after hitting any
shot, including one's own serve, in order to get
np on the next shot. The main attributes of a
ready position are flexed knees, weight slightly
ard and evenly distributed between both feet,
racket held directly in front of the body in the
and grip.

e two sequences of smaller figures show how,
a proper and alert position, the receiver can
to cover all possible serves in either court.

pation of shots and preparation for strokes depends on the whole range of senses, and not just ready muscles, or a willing mind, or a sharp eye. Total involvement of the senses is what makes a ready position good.

We can be more specific in defining a good, grooved set of grips —the second common denominator in the games of the great champions—and I can't stress enough the long-range significance of learning to grip correctly in your own game.

A gifted athlete, or particularly determined competitor, can hit shots effectively with a poor hold on the racket. Ilie Nastase has a bad backhand grip, believe it or not—his hand is too much on top of the racket—and he gets away with it because of native ability. But the vast majority of players would be unable to compensate for a grip defect. And the more ordinary your abilities are, the bigger the penalty you will pay for gripping your racket improperly.

I advocate playing the game with three different grips—a grip for hitting balls off the forehand, or right side of your body, including volleys and lobs; a grip for hitting all the backhand shots; and a serving grip, for hitting serves and smashes. We'll save discussion of the serving grip, which is a slight variation of the basic backhand grip, for a bit later. And we will discuss two interesting variations on the backhand grip, including the grip for the potentially devastating two-handed backhand shot, in the special section devoted to finding one's personal winning tennis style.

For now, examine the forehand and backhand grips that I recommend to see why they are productive of the controlled power desirable from each side. The illustrations on pages 26–27 show the hand linked to the racket handle for both grips, at key points in each stroke and from several vantage points. Left-handers must as usual bear with the text and pictures and read "left" for "right" in order to build their own grips correctly according to the instructions which follow.

In the forehand grip, the V formed by the thumb and index finger is lined up with the right-hand edge of the panel on the top of the racket handle. Note how this alignment puts the bulk of the hand *behind* the racket at the time of impact. Imagine the hand without the racket at that point and you may observe it is in an excellent position for hitting in a game of handball—or for spanking a toddler with an open palm. If the hand is rotated even slightly counter-clockwise, or left of this position, the same hitting action becomes more difficult to effect. One would have to flick the wrist a bit to bring the palm of the hand squarely into the handball, or the baby's bottom. We don't want such a variable in our forehand stroke because it would promote inconsistency.

In the backhand grip, the same V is lined up with the *left-hand* edge of the panel on top of the handle. All racket handles are made with eight panels, by the way, and when I refer to the "top" panel, I simply mean the one seen as "on top" by any player looking down at his racket in a good ready position.

Study the effect of the slight but immensely significant change in positioning of the hand for the backhand grip. During the interval of impact, the thumb and a good portion of the heel of the hand are behind the handle, supporting the racket and driving weight into the shot just as the hand does when in the correct grip on the forehand side. The thumb is the workhorse in the backhand grip. You should feel its pressure on the handle throughout the stroke. If you picture the hand without the racket at this point, you might think it belonged to a karate expert at work. But if the hand is rotated clockwise, or to the right of this position—back toward the forehand grip—the action resembles a feeble, back-of-the-hand-type slap.

A handball shot on the forehand side and a karate blow on the backhand side—those are farfetched but revealing analogies for the kind of stroking action encouraged in tennis by proper grips. They suggest strength, authority, and control from both sides. That's what we're after.

Anyone can hold the racket in the grips I've described, for they aren't mysterious, like fraternal handshakes, or unorthodox in any way. They are the grips most good tennis instructors try to impart to their pupils. The trouble is, most newcomers to the game find learning the grips a dull piece of business and get it behind them as soon as possible.

25

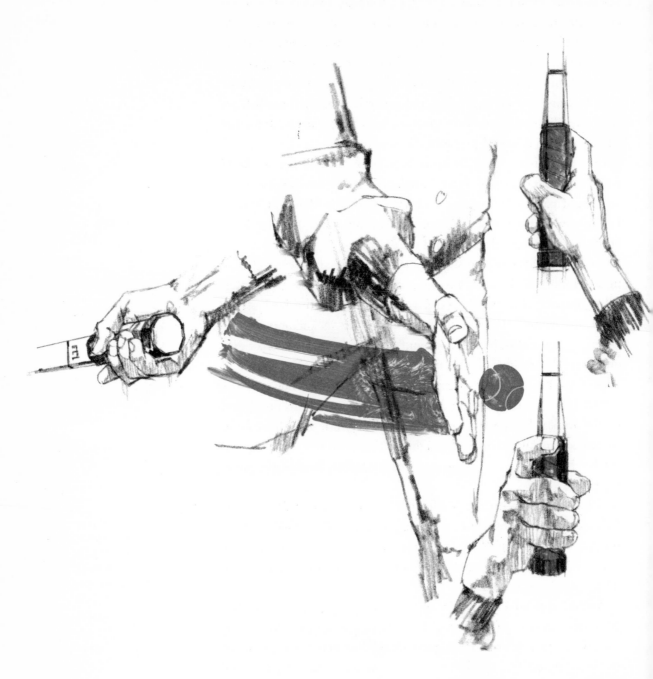

FOREHAND

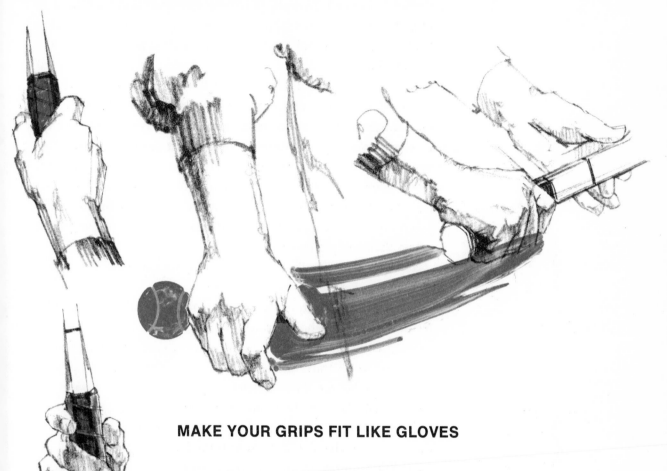

BACKHAND

MAKE YOUR GRIPS FIT LIKE GLOVES

Solid grips are indispensable to developing controlled power on the groundstrokes in tennis. Correctly made, they permit you to use your hand-and-forearm strength with maximum effectiveness, as though you were actually slapping the ball, on the forehand side, or giving it a karate blow with the heel of the hand, on the backhand side. Note that, for the forehand grip, the "V" formed by thumb and finger straddles the right edge of the racket handle (in the bird's-eye view) and that, for the backhand, the "V" straddles the left edge. Greater comfort and control are achieved when the first finger is extended (as shown in the worm's-eye view).

Furthermore, most players learn their groundstrokes in sequence rather than together. Unless you acquire both grips and both strokes at the same time, by practicing forehands and backhands in roughly equal amounts from the outset, you are likely to develop confidence and control on one side to the detriment of your progress on the other side.

Most players learn the forehand first. Those rare birds who learn the backhand first run into the same trouble, only in reverse. Introduce the No. 2 stroke later and—no matter what your teacher says to you, or you say to yourself—there will be a difficult period of adjustment. If you started on the forehand, the new backhand glove won't fit. You'll have that tentative feeling that American tourists get in Great Britain when they rent a car for the first time and try to negotiate the left side of the roads over there. Everything seems alien and perilous.

The problem usually resolves itself in one of two ways, both unsatisfactory:

Like a good student, you'll stick to that backhand grip. It will be technically correct, but it won't be psychologically correct, so you won't trust it, and you won't use it unless you're absolutely forced to, so you won't learn to trust it. You'll join the masses of players who are dyed-in-the-wool forehand-only players.

Or you'll cheat on that uncomfortable backhand grip until it feels *psychologically* correct. That is, your hand will centimeter its way around the handle back towards the forehand grip that you do trust. You won't go all the way back—just far enough to get rid of most of your anxieties. But it will be far enough to give you a technically *incorrect* backhand grip, and that will cause mechanical problems in the stroke itself. You'll have a backhand, but it will be weak and unreliable.

You may inquire at this point about players who hit forehands and backhands with the same grip—a Continental, or in-between, grip in which the hand is positioned so that the V between thumb and index finger bisects the panel on top of the racket. Top pros like Tony Roche, Tom Okker, and Bob Lutz all are one-grip players. Why not hold the racket their way and avoid all these learning problems? Let me first of all mention the hazards in copying the styles of highly skilled athletes who play tennis for a living. Their inborn abilities and years of repetitious practice permit them to overcome to a large degree any number of questionable features in their technique.

For most players, the one-grip method hurts the forehand too much on both groundstrokes and on volleys. The hand is not set fully behind the racket handle, as it is in the correct forehand grip, and so it is harder to generate power. True, Okker hits that powerful topspin forehand of his off the one grip. But what a wristy stroke it is—demanding phenomenal quickness and timing. No developing player or weekend player of even superior abilities could ever hit the shot with enough consistency to make it pay. Tony Roche has a justly feared backhand volley. With the one-grip method, backhands tend to be hit fairly well. But Tony's forehand volley isn't dangerous at all, at least not when put next to that of his longtime doubles partner, John Newcombe, who has a superb forehand grip. The only player I've ever seen hit a sizzling forehand volley with a backhand-type grip was Frank Sedgman. And that was because Frank had a wrist built like an iron vise. Bob Lutz is also unusually powerful through the forearms and wrists and that's why he gets away with one-grip tennis.

As far as the newcomer or weekend player goes, it boils down to this: The one-grip system neither adds nor subtracts substantially from your effectiveness on the backhand side. If all goes well, you will evolve into playing a strong defensive backhand whether you hold the racket in the backhand grip that I recommend or in an in-between grip.

But the one-grip system definitely would encourage weaker and more inconsistent shotmaking off your *forehand* side, both from the baseline and up at net, because it demands much more inherently risky wrist action. As we shall see shortly, it is that extra bit of power available off the forehand that can give the vast majority of players something to attack with. Why spoil the chance for a point-winner later on by compromising your grips at the start?

29

Making Your Grips Fit Like Gloves

It may be easier to convince newcomers of the long-range value in the two-grip system than it is to present a surefire method for acquiring good forehand and backhand grips at the same time.

But consider the following suggestions for achieving both technical and psychological correctness in the two grips.

PICK LARGEST RACKET HANDLE YOU CAN MANAGE

There's one good reason to use a racket with the largest possible handle for your hand size. The fatter the racket handle, the more space will exist between your forehand and backhand grip positions. So the better you may be able to identify and groove the different feelings of the two grips.

You don't have to be strong to handle a big-handled racket—it is not like using stiff-shafted clubs in golf, for example. You don't have to throw out your existing racket, either. Tennis shops can build up or reduce grip size in a jiffy for you for a small charge. Standard sizes on adult models begin at 4½ inches—the circumference of the handle as measured at its broadest part—and increase at ⅛-inch intervals up to 5½ inches. The tendency of most newcomers to the sport is to pick out rackets with smaller handles, because it bolsters their confidence in the ability to control the equipment. But you can be misled in this manner to the detriment of your game. If the handle is too small, it will come loose during shots, promote undue wristiness, and actually increase the work your hand has to do in holding on.

And those two different grip positions you're trying to learn won't contrast as sharply.

MEMORIZE THE GRIP POSITIONS

Aspiring magicians, I am told, put in long hours in front of mirrors working on their sleight-of-hand tricks. Good tennis grips are a kind of trick of manual dexterity, too, and it takes some of that magician's devotion to learn them.

Work on the grips in front of a mirror to be sure you line up the V of thumb and forefinger as I've described for both grips. This process also builds up your familiarity with the two grips. With enough repetition, the grip positions will begin to feel normal and

30

natural. There's no reason why beginners should expect to intuitively hold a tennis racket correctly—any more than a small child figures out a pair of scissors at the first go. But once you are shown how to hold the racket properly, and overcome your initial feeling of strangeness, it's up to you to practice the grips until they are second nature—a pair of gloves that fit so well you don't even know you have them on.

If molding your grips before the mirror gets wearisome, work on it while you're watching TV, or reading in bed.

GROOVE THE CHANGE OF GRIPS

The real trick comes in changing from one grip to the other quickly and smoothly, and back and forth again, as often as the tennis action requires. You can practice changing grips on your own to a certain degree, but your greatest progress in this neglected and often misunderstood technique will come in rallying with an instructor, practice partner, or ball machine. Many ball machines can be programmed to feed shots alternately to your left and right side, which is the ideal pattern for grooving the two grips and getting used to making the transition between them, as well as for practicing your basic groundstrokes.

Your grip-changing procedure will be the more effective if:

1. you make use of the free hand to help in the job, and

2. you make it a rule to start in the forehand grip, and stay in it or return to it after every shot.

Let me explain why these two refinements will add immeasurably to your gripping technique and, in time, to your entire game.

In the good ready position, the free hand helps support the racket in front of the body. In this neutral slot, the racket can be shifted with equal ease and speed into the forehand or the backhand backswing.

A right-hander in the ready position, then, would hold the racket in the forehand grip with the right hand, and lightly at the throat of the racket in the left hand—with the racket resting on the fingers of the left hand, and with the thumb either on the top panel or wrapped around.

When the ball comes to the forehand side, the left hand falls

31

free of the racket and that's about all. It helps your balance during the stroke, but that's not a role you really have to think about.

When the ball comes to the backhand side, the free hand happens to be in a position to aid preparation. Tug the racket promptly with the left hand and the backswing is underway. And the right hand has a moment's grace to slide over into the proper backhand grip. If the left hand were not holding the racket firmly at this stage, the right hand would have to support the racket at the same time it is groping for the correct grip, with the chances being against finding it every time. Early preparation for the shot would also be in doubt.

Now let me try to make clear why the forehand grip should be your base grip during play, and bear with me as I briefly jump ahead to matters relating to strokemaking rather than to gripping per se.

It takes more time to go from the backhand grip to the forehand grip than it does to go from the forehand grip to the backhand grip, principally because of the availability of the free hand to speed up things on the backhand side, but also because of the nature of the rotation. Also, the forehand stroke that we will be trying to develop is a naturally longer and somewhat more cumbersome stroke than is the type of backhand that you will use against the vast majority of balls hit to the backhand side. The power forehand takes more time to hit than the defensive backhand.

So, always waiting in the forehand grip during play is really a means for *equalizing* the preparation time required for each stroke. It does *not* hinder the development of a good backhand. Once you've got your grip changes down pat through practice, you'll always have time to hit backhands with the proper grip. If you did wait in the backhand grip during play, however, you would not always have time to get into the proper grip for hitting a good forehand.

From a tactical standpoint—and soon you will begin to appreciate the complex tactical dimension of this game—waiting in the forehand grip is advantageous because it creates more opportunities for you to hit aggressive shots. You'll be ready to attack any ball that comes remotely down the middle with your stronger shot, without the need of a grip change beforehand.

Let these be your guidelines for changing grips throughout the development of your basic baseline game:

* Hit a forehand, and remain in the forehand grip.
* Hit a backhand, and immediately *return* to the forehand grip.
* Always wait for serves in the forehand grip.
* After you hit your own serves (which will be with a modified backhand grip), always return to the forehand grip.

If you could always play against a practice machine that feeds ball after ball to the exact same spot in the court, it might be possible to overlook footwork and body positioning in introducing groundstrokes to new players. It would be enough to concentrate on the stroking motion itself.

However, as you will discover when you start practicing with your friends, balls come across the net to your side with an astonishing variety of angles, arcs, and speeds.

To begin to hit these infinitely varied bouncing balls back with any consistency, you must *set up* correctly, with your entire body, as well as *stroke* correctly, with your hand, arm, and racket.

Indeed, the setup aids the stroke to such an extent that I would be hard put to say where the setup ends and where the stroke begins, on any shot played off a bouncing ball.

I admit it is quite possible to hit tremendous shots when out of position and off balance—that's one of the things that makes tennis exciting. But in learning groundstrokes for the first time, if you do not set up right for each shot—or as close to right as you can depending on how and where you have to move to get to the ball—your chances of stroking well will be greatly reduced.

To standardize your setup on forehands and backhands, always strive to meet the ball in front of your forward foot, with your body

Standardize Your Strike Zone

33

USE YOUR FEET & KNEES TO MEET ALL BALLS IN YOUR STRIKE ZONE

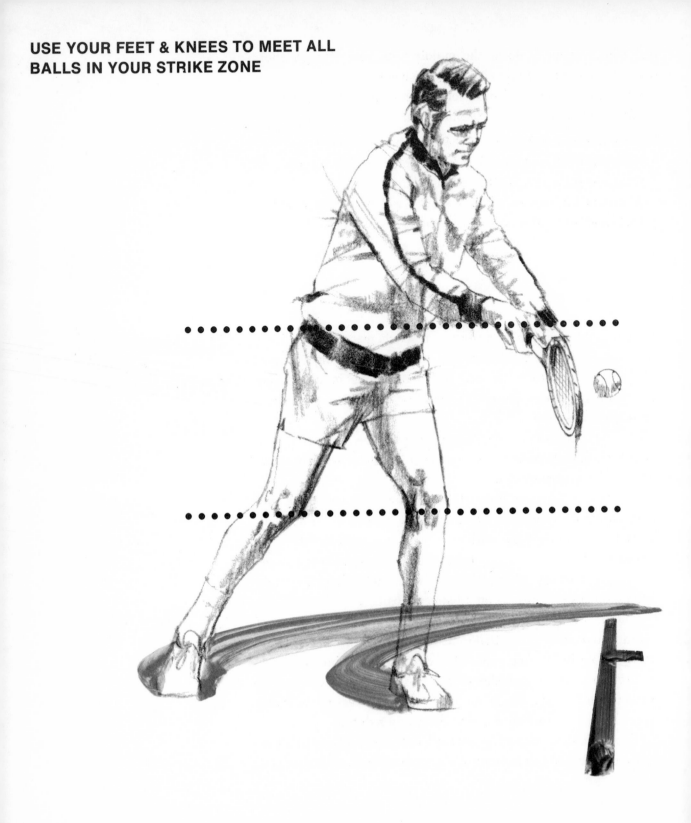

e most successful tennis players, at any level of play, are those who have learned
 hit their groundstrokes in basically the same way, every time they make a shot.
e grooved, automatic stroke produces greater consistency and fewer errors than
e invented, spur-of-the-moment shot.

At first you should make a special effort to meet all shots through your waist—so
at the relationship among arm, hand and racket remains about the same. Run
ck to catch high-bouncing balls on the way down (Fig. 1) in order to avoid
inging at shoulder-level, and until you've developed the
actions to catch balls on the rise before they've peaked. On
w-bouncing balls, use your knees more to lower your
tomatic stroke to the level of the shot (Fig. 2).

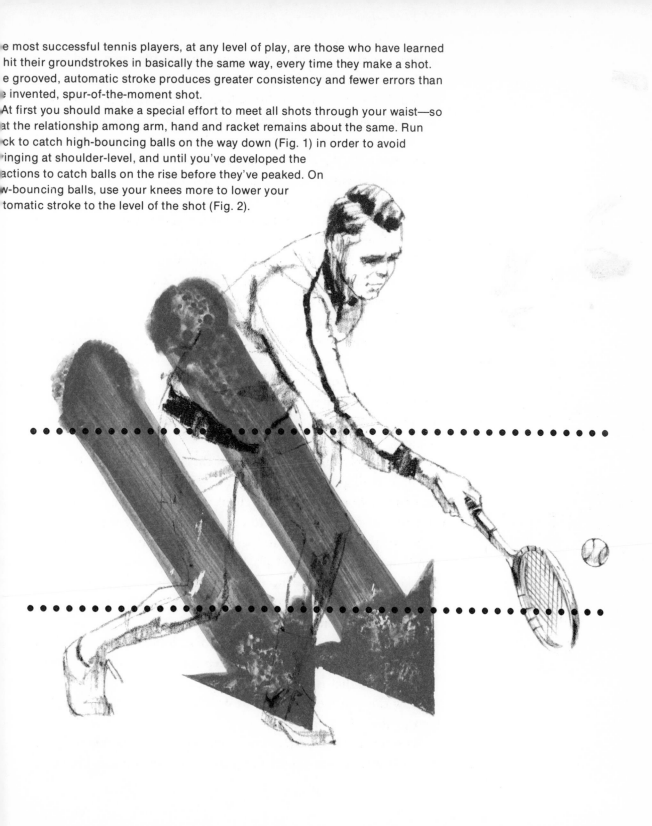

sideways to the net, and with your waistline at the same level as the ball when your racket hits it.

This is the best spot for the ball to be, in relation to your body, for you to swing comfortably and effectively. Setting up sideways to the intended line of flight of your shot makes it possible to shift your hips in the direction of your target when you make your stroke. This weight transfer allows you to generate power effortlessly.

The ideal hitting stance, then, is an exact 90-degree departure from the ideal ready position. Awaiting shots, you're face-on to the net. Executing shots, you're side-on to the net.

With your strike zone etched in your mind, you must then use your feet and knees so that you are able to meet the ball when it passes through that zone on all groundstrokes.

Your future tennis opponents, through a certain combination of skill, incompetence, and luck on their part, will avoid producing *any* shots that bounce up exactly into your strike zone. Instead, they will send you into the corners after balls, or hit some shots short and others deep, and some that bounce high and others that bounce hardly at all, or some straight at you and some at sharp angles.

The way to reduce the number of these variables—and they are intrinsic to all groundstroke exchanges—is through *proper footwork and knee action*. Again, an excellent model for moving to the ball in tennis would be a top guard in basketball staying with his man.

More specifically, by learning to anticipate from a good ready position where and how balls bounce in your backcourt, and by quickly performing the necessary legwork to assume the proper hitting stance in each case, you will be able to hit most shots approximately "through the waistline."

Let's say you're in your ready position, located dead center on your own baseline. A ball is hit deep into a corner and bounces up to a peak that is level with your shoulders.

How can you meet the ball at waistline level when in fact it is two or three feet *higher?*

By retreating behind the baseline far enough to be able to catch the ball *after* it has passed the peak of its bounce and begun its descent. In other words, *using your feet;* you must run to a spot that allows you to meet the ball as it drops through your hitting plane.

Now let's say a ball is hit short—in the area of your service line, which is 18 feet inside your court—and that it bounces up to a much shorter peak somewhere between knee and waist level.

This time, in order to hit the ball through your waistline, you must not only use your *feet* to get into the correct hitting stance, you must also use your *knees,* once you get there, as a kind of elevator, to bring your body down to the level of the shot.

Later in your development as a player, it will be possible and indeed desirable for you to make contact with balls in your strike zone *before* they've bounced to their peak. Hitting groundstrokes on the rise gives you more control over the point at hand because the ball gets back over the net sooner and usually with more pace on it.

For now, though, concentrate on meeting all low bouncing balls at the peak of their bounce and all high bouncing balls *after* the peak, doing all that you can with your lower body—your feet and knees—to make sure your strike zone remains the same.

I hope by relating body to ball in terms of the stroke in this manner, we are free to dispense with lengthy sermons on footwork, and with the various dance-step diagrams that generally go with such sermons. I do think, if you are striving to hit all shots at your waist level and in front of your forward foot, your preparatory movements will occur with less self-consciousness. You'll hop, skip, slide, and step according to the one thought of being able to push the button on your automatic stroke, rather than bending over to hit one shot, stretching up to hit another, falling over to hit still another, as though each bouncing ball demanded a special shot of its own.

It's the automatic stroke, not the improvised one, that ensures a durable ground game in tennis.

Low-to-High Swing for Topspin

A tennis ball weighs only two ounces, so, unless you hit it very softly, some degree of underspin or topspin has to be put on it to control its flight and keep it in the court. I recommend starting with topspin on both forehands and backhands because it yields a greater variety of aggressive shots.

The correct way to impart topspin is to swing the racket with a firm wrist from about knee level on the backswing to about shoulder level on the forward swing. This movement of the racket head on a rising path through your strike zone causes the racket strings to brush up and over the ball and get it spinning end over end in the direction of the target.

A much trickier way to get topspin is to hit the shot like a Ping-Pong player, by bringing the racket face up and over the ball with a flick of the wrist. This takes super athletic ability—to meet the ball at exactly the right spot—and an extra strong wrist. Not recommended.

The advantages of hitting with topspin are many. It allows you to hit the ball hard without sacrificing control. In fact it is a low-risk shot, once grooved. A good forehand or backhand hit with moderate topspin—we will not be striving for the extreme topspin of a Borg or a Guillermo Vilas—will produce a shot that travels in a half-moon trajectory, clearing the net by 3 to 4 feet and landing 2 to 3 feet inside the baseline. Thus, you can give the net a wide berth when you have the capability to hit groundstrokes with topspin, and still obtain excellent depth.

Tactically, topspin opens up the court for you against an opponent who plays in the backcourt, making it much easier for you to produce forcing shots and placements (outright winners crosscourt), and it gives you the weapon of the passing shot to use against the opponent who comes in to net to volley.

During rallys from the baseline, it allows you to hit a crosscourt shot hard enough from any position to carry your opponent somewhat out of court and so create a larger vacant area for you to hit to on your next shot. If you hit a chop or slice from the same position—shots with underspin rather than topspin—it would travel slower and your opponent would be likely to get to it in plenty of time. On some indoor surfaces, it would also bounce higher, making it even easier for the opponent to return. Generally, on thick carpets and on clay, underspin shots bounce low. Once your opponent is pulled wide by topspin, another topspin shot, either to the open corner or behind him as he moves to cover that open corner, will usually win the point. It will force an error by your opponent as he rushes his next effort—or he may not get to it at all.

If your opponent charges the net against you, you have three options in theory:

1. Get the ball by him by lobbing.
2. Get the ball by him by hitting down the line.
3. Get the ball by him by hitting crosscourt.

Without the topspin capability, however, option No. 3 won't exist. The ball won't be traveling fast enough off a slice to stave off interception by a volley. Option No. 2 won't be as attractive, either, for your opponent, knowing your crosscourt shot is a slice that he can catch up with, will be ready for your down-the-line shot.

There are other examples of topspin's usefulness, both in attack and in counterattack—and also in the doubles game, where it is invaluable on the return of serve—and we'll get to them later. At this stage, I've merely tried to suggest the versatility of the shot so as to motivate you to work seriously toward producing topspin off both groundstrokes.

You'll discover in practice sessions, and more particularly in actual matches when opponents are doing their best to confound you, that most balls hit to your backhand side will bounce either too high or too low to easily hit them back with a topspin-producing low-to-high stroke, and you'll have to hit an underspin-producing slice instead.

Don't worry about that for now. The chance to hit topspin on only a few backhands per match is well worth striving for, as a matter of fact. Furthermore, it is vital to practice the groundstrokes as one so that you are comfortable and confident in both grips and in changing from one grip to the other, and you can't do this if you have different stroking motions in mind for either side. So many club players today are one-sided—able to hit forehands but not

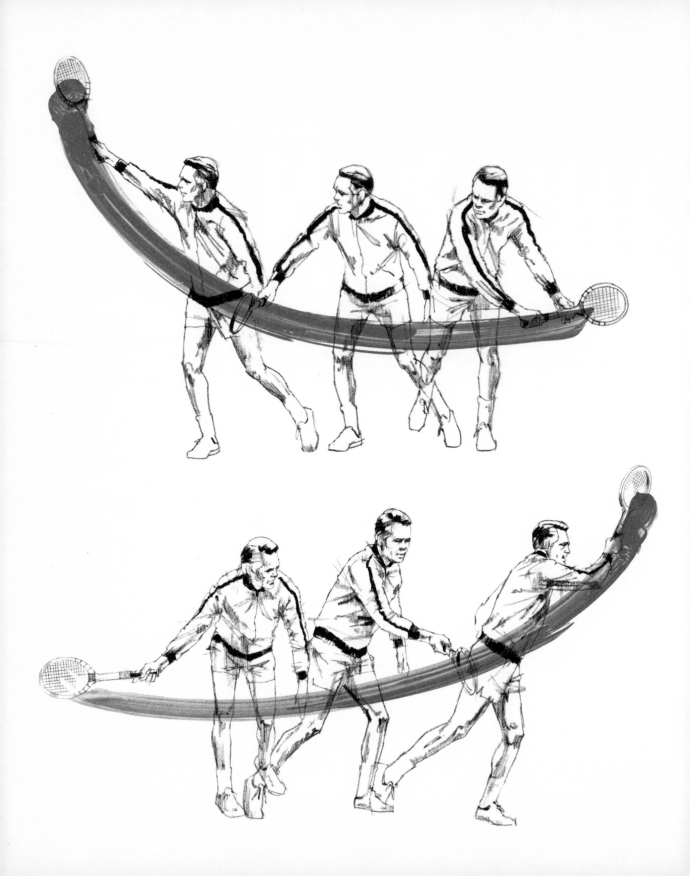

SWING LOW TO HIGH

Aggressive topspin shots can be produced effortlessly from both forehand and backhand sides if you hold the racket in the correct grip, and swing with a firm wrist from a low position (at about knee level at the start of the forward swing) to a high position (at about shoulder level or higher on the follow-through). No "rolling over" of the wrist is necessary or, indeed, desirable in the course of stroking in order to produce this spin; the path of the racket itself does the job.

The simple and compact low-to-high stroking motion is one which players should try to groove, or "automate," right from the start. Note that the ball is met well in front of the forward foot (middle figure in each sequence) on both forehand and backhand.

Smooth Weight Transfer for Pace

backhands, as a rule—because early in their development they made the mistake of emphasizing the differences in groundstrokes, rather than the similarities. At this stage, what forehands and backhands have in common is much more important than how they differ.

Pace refers to the speed of the ball after it has bounced and it is a direct result of getting a lot of body weight into the shot. (It is also more easily achieved when using a *heavy* racket, as will be explained later.) You can hit a ball fast by a whipping motion of arm, wrist, and racket, but it won't have pace unless you step into the shot with the weight of your body behind the shot. And without pace, the shot will be easier to hit back once it has bounced.

Sometimes you'll hear reference to a "heavy ball." Players who generate a lot of pace on their shots actually make the ball feel a lot heavier than its two ounces when you get your racket on it. Segura's forehand and Budge's backhand generated so much pace that unless you gripped extra firmly, their shots would knock the racket out of your hand.

Players who hit with topspin generally develop more pace on their shots than players who hit with underspin. But if the topspin is extreme—as in the groundstrokes of Laver, Borg, and Vilas—the pace is not as hard to handle.

Underspin players can also generate pace, however, Ken Rosewall's backhand slice being the outstanding example.

A smooth swing with a lot of body weight behind it produces pace. Ask a pro after a match how he managed to hit the ball so hard and he may look surprised—often he won't be aware just how much pace he's generating. But a hard swing with no body weight produces very little pace.

A lot of the walking wounded on our tennis courts today are those who make use of their weight exclusively to keep their tennis outfits on—and who operate the racket with only their arms. You must *shift* your weight in the direction you are hitting the ball, not just plant it, to absorb the force directed against your racket and to return the ball forcefully, *and without strain or injury to your hand, wrist, elbow, arm, or shoulder.*

If an arm-only stroke doesn't actually hurt you, it will certainly wear you down before any typical match is over. And for all its outwardly mighty look, it does not produce the consistency and control you want in your ground game.

When you properly coordinate the shifting of your weight with stroking through your hitting plane, you only have to exert half as much effort to be a hard hitter. That's why youngsters and many women players should pay particular attention to this fundamental to all good strokes. The bones and muscles in your arms may be smaller, but your shots don't have to be punier. The late Maureen Connolly Brinker, one of the tiniest champions in the history of the game, was able to generate more power on her forehands than many of today's top *men* pros! Her secret was her exceptionally well-timed transfer of weight.

The weight transfer is an integral part of the backswing, forward swing, and finish—the three phases of every stroke—and must be learned and practiced in that framework. There's less to be gained in shifting your weight if you're out of position when the ball comes up, or if you're hitting it too late, or if you don't flex your knees to provide a kind of chassis for the transfer. In other words, this fundamental should be at work throughout.

Try shifting weight without actually hitting balls for a time. Concentrate on linking the act of taking the racket back with the establishment of the bulk of your body weight on the back foot in your stance. That sets the stage for the transfer. Then work on linking the actual shifting forward of the weight with the movement of the racket through your hitting area. Once you have your timing down, you'll be getting pace on your shots without swinging hard at all.

Backswing, Forward Swing, Finish

Let's examine the groundstrokes in their three different operational phases of backswing, forward swing, and finish.

I'll take them from the ready position on through the completion of the basic stroke, and back to the ready position again.

To prevent confusion, I'll point out where and how the strokes differ in feeling and execution. Don't fail to use the identical stroking motion for each of them, though. So that the strings brush up on the ball during the interval of impact and give you the topspin you want on the shot, always bring the racket on a path from knee level on the backswing to above eye level on the followthrough. You should finish so that the hand holding your racket is at least at about the level of your eyes and the racket itself is higher than that. As you'll see a bit later, the higher the finish the more topspin is obtained.

In practice of the strokes, remember to mix forehands and backhands in every session and in equal amounts, so that you feel at home hitting from both sides, and so that you get used to a smooth change of grips.

1. BACKSWING

During the backswing, the racket is brought into the hitting position at the same time as the body gets into the hitting stance. The pivot of the body helps you get the racket back.

You are already in the forehand grip in your ready position, so if you see that the ball is going to come to the right side, let the free hand fall away from the racket and take the racket straight back.

If the ball comes to the left side, use the free hand as a helping hand to pull the racket back at the same time as you find your backhand grip.

Use of the free hand in this manner promotes greater uniformity in the backswings on the backhand side, incidentally. Forehands tend to wander more without that standardizing influence.

Nevertheless, on both sides the goal is to execute the simplest possible backswing, one that places the racket in its knee-high hitting position behind you A.S.A.P. Later you'll discover it's natural to take the racket back in a bit of a loop, but the simplest way

44

for beginners to make the backswing is to bring the racket from the ready position straight back to knee-level as they pivot.

Starting the backswing quickly is the *only* way to be sure you'll get the racket forward again in time to meet the ball early enough in its flight to produce a forceful shot off it.

It takes no great feat of coordination to start the racket back promptly, only belief in the value of this action, and a bit of character and persistence in making it an habitual response. Tell yourself to concentrate on moving the racket back the moment you determine the direction the ball is coming, after it has left your opponent's racket. Try to react before the ball crosses the net, and by all means react before the ball has actually bounced. You'd be surprised how many players of some experience are guilty of waiting as late as that.

The quick and direct backswing works whether you have to run to get to the ball or merely pivot into a good hitting stance. It's more important to get it back quickly when there's less time to prepare, obviously, but what's wrong with getting it back as quickly as possible every time? And if you have to take several steps to get into your hitting stance, what's so hard about taking the racket back on your way, rather than waiting until you get there and then jerking it back?

When you don't swing the racket back quickly, you get into the rut of inventing shots every time the ball comes to you. You're playing with shots that you haven't practiced.

2. FORWARD SWING

During the forward swing, the racket moves on a rising path into the strike zone to meet the ball, in time with a full weight transfer.

One of the game's top teachers, John Gardiner, likens the position of the arm, wrist, and shoulder on the forward swing in the forehand to that of the arm when you're carrying a heavy suitcase. If you keep the arm perfectly straight for either activity, you'll get tired very quickly. So you bend the arm slightly at the elbow to make the suitcase easier to carry. Same thing when you hit the forehand. It's a natural element in the stroke that you shouldn't have to think about.

45

On the backhand, however, the arm must straighten completely when you bring the racket into the strike zone, in order to transfer the power generated on your backswing and pivot. Note that the strike zone is located closer to the net for the backhand than it is for the forehand. Since the hitting arm is on the side near the net, it needs that additional four to six inches up front to operate fluidly. Meet the ball too late on the backhand side, and the arm will still be bent at the elbow, and all your power will be lost. That's why you can't let a ball get behind you on the backhand side—as you often can on the forehand—and still hope to pull it off. Timing the weight transfer correctly is slightly different for forehands and backhands because of that.

Stepping out toward the oncoming ball is indispensable to a good weight transfer on the backhand side.

It's important to practice the forehand complete with step, too. In reality you don't *have* to take that step to get your weight into the shot on forehands. In fact, the only time you'll ever see a textbook forehand in action at the highest level of play is when a player runs around his backhand to hit an aggressive forehand. That's the only time you should copy a top pro's forehand style, because all the other forehands are hit on the run, off balance and in an open stance—with feet and shoulders facing the net rather than side-on to the net as is ideal *and as is essential* in first learning the stroke.

Maintaining a firm wrist through the strike zone for *both* strokes helps to keep the racket strings in contact with the ball for a longer period of time, and so strengthens the brushing-up action on the ball. There should be no variation here from either side. I like the old teaching term "collect" to describe the action of the racket in the hitting area. The racket *collects* the ball—implying that, if only for a brief interval of time, you're holding onto the ball with those strings.

In order to be sure the wrist is firm at impact, which makes possible the collecting of the ball, I advocate keeping it firm throughout the backswing, at least now at the outset of groundstroke development. Eventually, you'll find that breaking the wrist somewhat as you take the racket back occurs naturally, especially on the forehand side. But until you have the habit of keeping the wrist firm through impact, it's dangerous to relax beforehand.

Breaking the wrist actually makes it easier to get the racket back quickly—but often at the expense of the proper movement of your lower body. It's easy to get lazy but a bent wrist can't make for a good hitting stance, and it ruins the forward swing entirely. Make your wrist a firm link between forearm and racket handle at every stage of the stroke. Remember, players of ordinary athletic ability with wristy strokes make sensational shots every once in a while—and errors the rest of the time.

3. FINISH

During the followthrough, the body is obliged to finish the business started on the backswing and forward swing. It's largely a *reactive* process, but it can tell you as much about how well you've executed the stroke as the results of the shot itself. So paying attention to your finish on every shot is an important part of the job of grooving groundstrokes correctly.

Most fences that enclose tennis courts are ten feet high. If you can finish a forehand or a backhand stroke with your racket extended out in the direction of the top of that fence, your followthrough will be good. The racket will be at above your eye level, indicating you've completed the low-to-high stroking action necessary to impart topspin. The hitting arm will be nearly straight, showing you've swung through the strike zone without fear of going long or overhitting. And 90 percent of your body weight will be on the front foot, showing you've made a pace-producing transfer.

On the forehand, it may feel a bit stiff and awkward at first to extend the racket to shoulder height, but it's what you should strive for. If you swing the racket more around your body at waist level, you'll pull the ball into the net or wide into the alley. Instead of brushing up on the ball, you'll smother it with the racket face, forcing the ball down and to the left.

The flowing backhand finish is more natural. Don't be alarmed if you sense a bit of hand action near the end of the stroke. I've stressed the need for a firm wrist up to this point, but all good backhands seem to finish with a slight wrist flip. It's a sign that you've lifted up on the ball properly.

The untutored player may have done everything right up to then, but now his groundstroke disintegrates into what it really is—either a *poke*, or a *push*. His short followthrough might be said to show a desire to bring the racket back to the body as soon as possible—as though he were ashamed of it.

In comparison, the good player seems to continue stroking the ball long after it has left his racket strings. His full finish might be said to reveal a desire to get the racket out as far as possible toward the target for that particular shot.

It is in developing this sense of keeping the strings on the ball throughout your strike zone that you really begin to complete your mastery of groundstrokes. A firm grip, a smooth weight shift, and a picture in your mind of swinging the racket head out toward the top of the fence—all of these will help you sustain the brushing action of the racket strings on the ball.

Once you've completed the followthrough, quickly resume your ready position.

If you've hit a forehand, stay in the forehand grip and return to the ready position.

If you've hit a backhand, change back to the forehand grip as you resume the ready position.

After you've worked on groundstrokes faithfully as suggested for a time, and as you begin to trade more shots with would-be opponents than you do with cooperative instructors, parents, friends, or ball-tossing machines, an important change occurs.

What might be called the "adversary factor" nurtures the emergence of an offensive role for the forehand, and a defensive role for the backhand.

The strokes become as different from each other in personality and purpose as the hook and the jab in boxing, or the drive and the wedge shot in golf, or the home run and the single in baseball.

Let's look at the forehand first.

On your forehand side, you'll notice that taking the racket straight back to knee level is too much of a chore. It's a rather muscular sort of backswing and when you do it constantly, you get tired. Without even realizing it, you're likely to start bringing the racket back in a bit of a loop or arc, rather than directly back. The racket will end up at knee level but it will get there along a more circular path.

The addition of the loop helps the forehand stroke in two ways.

First, it eases the job of taking the racket back. The arm remains more relaxed, so you can develop more rhythm in stroking from that side. With rhythm comes better timing and greater confidence.

Second, since the racket head now travels on a *longer* path, it automatically gathers more speed and potential power to deliver to the ball. The more time there is to prepare, the bigger the loop can be (within reasonable limits) and the greater the potential for generating topspin.

This is a logical development in mastery of strokemaking technique, and not an arbitrary tip on strategy from an old forehand player. The fact is, no matter how much time and effort might go into the practice of the backhand stroke, the vast majority of players are not going to be able to hit very many offensive backhands in competition. But point-winning forehands are within reach of *all* players, no matter what the level of their strength and athletic skill.

Let's look at this "hook-and-jab" development more closely, **49**

Ground-strokes Applied: Emergence of Your Power Forehand

Several factors stimulate development of the forehand as the point-winning shot, or at least the more offensive of the two groundstrokes, in the games of the vast majority of players. Players feel more security in the grip itself, and are naturally more confident in swinging from the right side of the body. Two other factors are shown here.

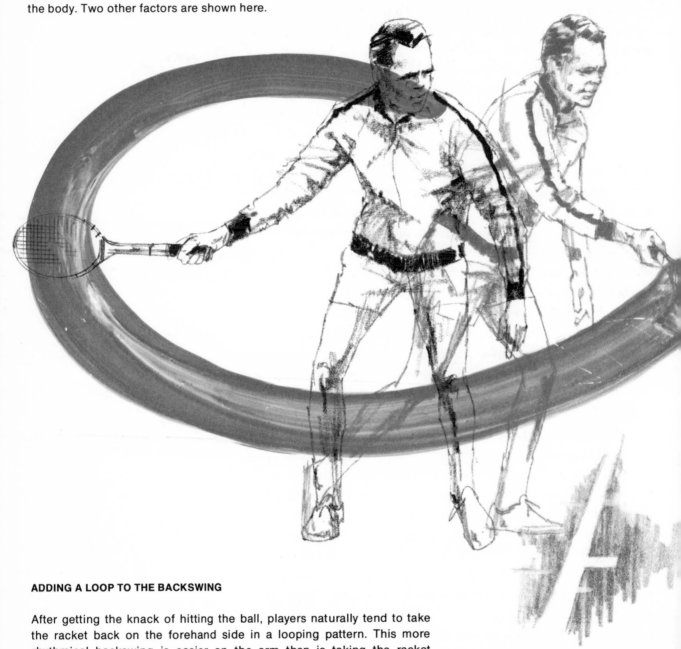

ADDING A LOOP TO THE BACKSWING

After getting the knack of hitting the ball, players naturally tend to take the racket back on the forehand side in a looping pattern. This more rhythmical backswing is easier on the arm than is taking the racket straight back. The lengthening of the swing arc generates more speed on the forward swing, which automatically creates more power on the shot.

TING HARD FROM AN OPEN STANCE

ehands can be hit late and from an open stance, unlike backhands, because the ket is held by the hand that is farther away from the oncoming shot, so there is re time to hit and still get some body weight in the shot. If the ball gets past the ward foot on the backhand side, the resultant shot must be weak.

because it is the foundation for solid and varied tactical play from the baseline, and it paves the way for building an effective net game later on as well.

With increased experience and confidence, you'll also gain more versatility in *directing* your forehands. Depth, rather than direction, has been the attribute we've stressed in shotmaking so far. But once an adversary appears on the court, direction looms in importance. The most elemental tactical impulse in the game, in fact, is to "hit 'em where they ain't." (That's why, as mentioned earlier, practice sessions should never be spent trading shots down the middle—such exchanges bear no resemblance to actual competition.)

Anyway, the reason you will develop a knack both for hitting the ball away from your opponent *crosscourt*—across the net at the middle—and in hitting it away from him *down the line*—across the net near either sideline—with your *forehand* much more easily than with your backhand is that the racket face and the ball are lined up for a longer interval on the forehand stroke, and so you get more flexibility in timing the shot. If you let the ball get past your front foot and into your body on the backhand side, you're dead. But you've got your strong arm behind your racket on the forehand side. You can meet the ball early, to send it crosscourt, or late, to send it down the line, with almost equal facility and without losing control.

Taken together, the increased power—thanks to the longer arm motion—and the broader target range—thanks to the chance to vary the timing of the hit—transform the forehand into an attacking stroke. Now you can produce shots that get back across the net extra fast, giving the opponent less time to get ready for them, and to exploit corners left open, making the opponent run more and perhaps hit off balance.

The amount of topspin produced off the power forehand can be increased by exaggerating the high finish on the stroke. This will happen almost instinctively if you are going for a little extra on the shot, as you might do to pass a net-rushing opponent crosscourt, or if you are attempting an aggressive shot from a deep position—a low-percentage shot but one you might try in certain relatively rare tactical situations. In any case, there is more *vertical lift* in the followthrough for a heavy topspin forehand. The racket finishes not only higher, but *closer to the body*—as though you are lifting the racket almost straight up through the impact area. The extra topspin produced allows you to hit the ball extremely hard and still keep it in bounds.

The power forehand, with or without the extra vertical lift, can only be hit when you have time to set up for the shot properly. There are many times when you must hit the forehand more defensively, as we'll try to make clear shortly. But once you understand that there is this rich potential for attack on the forehand side, you'll work harder to create the conditions in which you *do* have time to set up for the forehand.

Specifically, you'll always wait for serves, and for the next shots during rallys, in the good ready position and in the forehand grip—so you give yourself the best chance to set up in time to take the longer swing the power forehand requires, when the serve or shot does come to your forehand. And you'll create forehand shots out of serves or shots to your backhand that aren't wide enough or deep enough, by running around the ball to take it on the forehand side.

On the backhand side, extra power is not so easy to come by because of the nature of the majority of most balls that come to that side. In fact, you will find yourself confronted with a variety of shots that sorely test the low-to-high stroking motion you've been practicing.

Don't blame this on your good backhand grip, or your preparation, or your early work in trying to develop topspin from the backhand side.

The problem is outside your control. Backhands hit to backhands generally come in slow and high, bouncing up above waist level. That's because most of your adversaries won't be able to hit their

Ground-strokes Applied: All-Purpose Slice

backhands with topspin, either, so will produce purely defensive shots from that side. Forehands hit to backhands are usually attacking shots and generally come in low or fast or both.

The point is, neither of these commonly occurring shots to your backhand puts the ball where you can conveniently get to it with your topspin stroke.

If the ball comes in fast off a forehand, you won't have time to get your racket back far enough. If it comes in low, fast or slow, you won't be able to get the racket below the ball—unless you dig out part of the court doing it.

True, if the shot is a high-bouncer off a backhand, you can run back and set up to meet the ball after it's dropped from its peak and into the strike zone, in which case you would be able to employ the topspin backhand stroke you've been practicing.

But no matter how quick or energetic you are, you're going to get tired of doing that. It was important to catch the ball through the waistline during the initial stages of groundstroke development, because it helped you to mold a good backhand grip, get used to backhand footwork, and learn to swing at the ball on that side freely and with confidence.

Now, however, it would be unrealistic to expect you always to retreat to catch backhands at just the right height—and unsafe to uncork your topspin when the odds are against your succeeding even if you happen to be a gifted athlete.

There's a higher percentage shot for getting the ball back, in these situations, and it's the slice, or underspin backhand.

The slice depends on the same good backhand grip, but preparation is simpler and takes less time. The backswing is shorter and so is the followthrough. The racket travels on a high-to-low plane, a high-to-high plane, or a low-to-low plane, depending on the bounce of the ball, as contrasted with the low-to-high plane productive of topspin. Instead of the racket strings brushing up on the ball, they brush down and through it, causing the ball to spin opposite to the direction of its flight, with underspin, or backspin. There is less weight transfer in the slice and correspondingly less pace. The sliced ball travels with a somewhat less marked trajectory than the half-

THE ALL-PURPOSE SLICE BACKHAND

Players must content themselves with hitting many defensive, or underspin, shots from the backhand side because the topspin-producing low-to-high backhand can't be used against the majority of shots hit to that side. A hard or low-bouncing shot (Fig. 1), as would be produced by an opponent attacking with a forehand, doesn't give enough time to take a full swing. The slower high-bouncing shot (Fig. 2), as would be produced by an opponent hitting a defensive backhand, forces you to meet the ball too high to brush up and over it. Hence, the defensive backhand, with its shorter backswing and underspin-producing racket action during the interval of impact, emerges as an important stroke.

moon arc created by the topspin shot, and drops sharply because it runs out of steam. It's easier to make the shot crosscourt than down the line, but that is not a significant tactical shortcoming in rallying. In fact, if you're a right-hander hitting to another right-hander, you'll be slicing the ball into the opponent's backhand, and if you place it deep enough, it can be as effective as a forcing shot with your power forehand.

There are bonuses in mastering the underspin backhand.

One is tactical—it gives you the wherewithal for a good backhand approach shot. The weight transfer on the slice tends to carry you in the direction of the net more so than the transfer as it normally occurs in the topspin forehand, where the weight is nailed to the ground for a longer time after impact. So while the topspin shot may be hit harder, the underspin backhand gives you a couple of steps' headstart in reaching an aggressive position at net.

The other bonus is that, by learning the slice's more compact stroking motion and its undercutting action of racket strings on ball, you also acquire the basis for two other important shots in tennis—the backhand volley and the defensive lob. In terms of mechanics of grip and execution, the slice, the backhand volley, and the defensive lob are practically identical. Once you develop the slice, you'll be able to pick up the other two shots quickly and correctly. This fact alone should give players more incentive for working hard on grooving the underspin backhand.

In the meantime, don't throw your topspin backhand in the ashcan. There will be times when the ball does indeed bounce right where you want it and you'll have time to play the shot you started with from that side. It will come in handy particularly as a passing shot against an opponent rushing net against you. It will also be valuable as a weapon in doubles play, where the presence of the opponent's partner at the net puts a premium on accurate short crosscourt shots that carry topspin.

Realistically, however, you will seldom be able to unleash the topspin backhand safely. So the sensible thing to do is use that slice to keep the ball in play and to set up opportunities for the
forehand—with its greater range of offensive shots—to go to work.

There are three elementary laws governing the ground game in tennis. They are the cornerstone of a sound tactical approach from the baseline. It is no good hitting forehands and backhands in matches unless you understand them, become convinced of their validity, and are willing to shape your pattern of play according to them.

This rule actually covers all the shots, not just groundstrokes. Tennis is too hard a game for it to be otherwise. Keep track of the mistakes made during a match on TV between top players. You'll find that the winner invariably is the player who made fewer mistakes. A player may hit more great shots—more placements—but still lose the match in straight sets because he's also made more mistakes than the opponent.

The basic forehand, producing shots with a degree of topspin on it, is designed for power—for sending balls back over the net hard and fast. The basic backhand, producing shots with a degree of underspin, is designed for control—for sending balls over the net more slowly and with less chance of error.

From a tactical point of view, then, you are more likely to be able to hit shots for winners when you have a chance to use your forehand. So when a ball comes to your forehand, the possibility of going on the offensive should occur to you. Or when you know you need to go on the offensive, you should think "forehand" and look for the opportunity to use that stroke.

The same sort of tactical reasoning—a habit of mind that will gradually develop in your game—applies to the backhand. When a ball comes to your backhand, you should realize that your percentage effort from that side is a controlled shot to keep the ball in play. Trying to hit a string of winners from the backhand side would indicate an unrealistic idea of your shotmaking capability from that side.

So while the forehand may be the home run stroke in tennis, it's really easier, with the backhand, to hit singles.

There have been successful players whose strokes did not con-

Percentage Play from the Baseline

MORE POINTS ARE LOST ON ERRORS THAN WON ON PLACEMENTS

THE SIDE TO WHICH THE BALL COMES DICTATES THE TYPE OF SHOT YOU CAN PLAY EFFECTIVELY

57

form to this profile, but they're a tiny minority. Most newcomers to tennis will be better off to groom their forehand for the power shots and the backhand for the shots that will keep the ball in play when under attack themselves.

THE DEPTH TO WHICH THE BALL COMES DICTATES THE TYPE OF SHOT YOU CAN PLAY

From my observation of players at the club level, and also of a good number of pros out on the circuit, this is the rule most commonly ignored or misunderstood. The single biggest cause of errors in tennis is trying to do something with a shot when you're not in position to justify the effort. Percentage tennis boils down to knowing the time and place to play safely, to hit forcing shots, and to go for winners.

Divide the backcourt area into the STOP, CAUTION, and GO zones portrayed in the illustration on page 60. If you form the mental habit of relating where you find yourself on the court to the realistic shot options available to you in each zone, you won't go for winners when it is dangerous to do so, so you'll cut down dramatically on foolish errors. And you will exploit situations which are advantageous.

When the ball catches you back in the red-light zone, there's not much you can do with the shot no matter how good you are. Tell yourself, "I'm not going to win the point on this one, so I'll just keep it in play."

Your main goal is to get the ball back deep—into the opponent's red-light zone. Otherwise he may be able to attack you on the next play. Clear the net by four to six feet and don't flirt with the sidelines. Hit it down the middle or deep crosscourt. Hit it down the line to attack the other player's backhand unless you are on the run and can't stop to get back in time to protect your court.

There are two red-zone shots that require some additional explanation.

A high-bouncing ball—one that reaches its peak at shoulder level or higher—almost invariably catches you behind your baseline deep in your red-light zone. It looks easy because of its height, but players frequently hit it into the net, or short, permitting an opponent to play aggressively on the next shot.

58

An optical illusion seems to work itself on the player driven behind his own baseline. The extra distance your own shot must travel doesn't register, and the firmness and length of stroke required is missing from the reply. You think you're going to hit the ball well into the opponent's backcourt, and instead it bounces at his service line.

So I find that it's necessary to deliberately aim long on this shot. I suggest that you mentally pick out a spot some three or four feet *beyond* the other player's baseline and tell yourself that's where you want the ball to bounce. Then you'll be forced to hit the shot with plenty of firmness and followthrough, and it will clear the net by a healthy margin and land nice and deep. For every foot you're driven back of your baseline, add a foot to the distance you want to clear the net, to be sure you get depth.

Another tricky shot in the red-light zone is an extremely wide ball. Anytime you have to run to the sideline or off the court to catch up with a shot, you're not going to have time to set up and stroke fully. Take your racket no farther back than your shoulder as you move to the ball. Stroke through the ball from that limited windup and you'll get the feeling you're *shoving* the ball across the net. Actually you'll be hitting it with a short volley-type stroke.

Hit all wide balls back *crosscourt* rather than down the line. If you hit down the line, your momentum would carry you right off the court after making the shot, leaving a large sector for your opponent to attack on his next play, and pretty soon he would have you on a yo-yo. Hitting crosscourt helps to avoid this situation because the motion of the crosscourt stroke tends to arrest your momentum out of the court and so makes it possible for you to recover the center of your side more quickly. Naturally, if the opponent comes to net on you in this situation, there's nothing wrong with trying a passing shot down the line.

When the ball catches you in the yellow zone, play the next shot with *caution*.

If the ball comes from the center of the court, to your forehand or your backhand, hit it back down the line in order to be able to cover the next shot.

PERCENTAGE TENNIS IS KNOWING WHEN TO TRY WHAT

Percentage tennis means making moves and playing shots according to a realistic assessment of your skills and stamina, your location on the court, the type of shot played by your opponent—particularly its *height* when it gets to you—and your present competitive position in the match. Percentage players know what they can and can't do and develop a kind of "automatic signal" system to put that knowledge to work for them on the tennis court, without even thinking about it.

A simple way to begin to develop your own system is illustrated here. As in the upper court view, establish the spot in the court where you can stand and enjoy a view of the opposing baseline that is not obstructed by the net. Regard the area behind that spot as your STOP or RED-LIGHT ZONE. When an opponent's shot catches you in this zone, play the ball back defensively; don't try anything fancy.

Mark off a section in *front* of the spot that is 6 to 7' in depth, or about three racket lengths as shown in the two lower court views. Any time you find yourself in this CAUTION ZONE, choose your shot according to which side the ball comes to, how fast it's traveling and how high it bounces. Only if the ball bounces *above* net height to your stronger forehand side, say, should you consider playing an attacking shot. If it bounces low or fast or to the backhand (assuming that is your weaker stroke), then stay on caution and just keep the ball in play.

Mark off another section of about the same depth in front of your caution zone to establish your GO or GREEN-LIGHT ZONE. This is the area in which you ought to be able to play the majority of your groundstrokes, as approaches (behind which you can come to net to volley) or as placements (outright winners). Only if the short ball bounces *below* net height should you have to go back on caution.

The tall player's apparent advantage over the short player is considerably reduced and in many cases taken away when the short player has more strokemaking skill, and—as is usually the case—when the short player has greater speed and mobility. In other words, if you're about 5'7" and still relatively new to the game, your zones should be approximately as shown here for the 5'7" player. But if you are of average quickness and if you improve in the game, you will gradually be able to play more offensively from deeper in the court, until your zones are approximately as shown here for the 6'1" player.

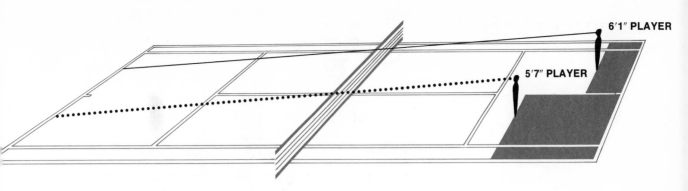

6'1" PLAYER

5'7" PLAYER

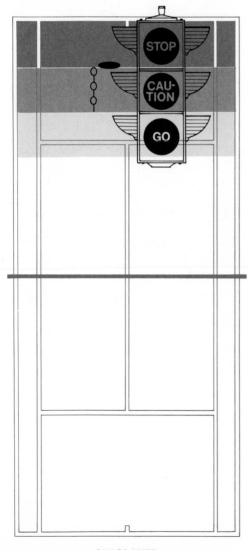

6'1" PLAYER **5'7" PLAYER**

PERCENTAGE TACTICS FROM THE BASELINE

Fig. 1 If the ball catches you this far back in your STOP ZONE, play the ball back extra safely. Clear the net by 6 to 8′ to get depth on the shot. If the opponent has come to net on you, lob.

Fig. 2 If a ball catches you wide and deep, it should be played back safely crosscourt (assuming the other player has remained at the baseline).

Fig. 3 A forcing shot can be hit from your CAUTION ZONE only if the ball bounces high and comes to your strong side.

Fig. 4 The short ball should be exploited by hitting an approach down the line and following it in to net. If the ball is sitting pretty above net level, it can be hit for a placement.

If the ball comes from down the line, hit a short crosscourt shot, using the corner of the service box as your target. This forces the opponent to run wide to retrieve the ball, leaving behind him a large vacant area for you to attack on the next shot.

This short crosscourt shot affords the best chance to go for winners—if you can hit it hard enough. On the forehand side, you may have the ability to do this. On the backhand side, your best bet may be to slice it crosscourt.

If the ball comes from crosscourt to your forehand in this yellow zone, a hard, down-the-line shot may win the point for you outright, too.

Generally, then, if the ball bounces high to your forehand when you're in the yellow zone, abandon caution and hit away. Otherwise, look for a chance to play the shot that forces your opponent out of position.

When the ball comes to you in your green-light zone, you're sitting pretty. Don't get cocky, though. Take your best shot on anything that bounces higher than net level. But if the ball bounces below the net, switch the caution light back on and play the ball back safely.

Most players make the mistake of overhitting when they're in their green-light zone. With a normal full groundstroke at this close range, you're likely to send the ball into the net or way out on the other side.

That's why the short ball should be handled with a shorter stroke even though you may be going for a winner. Take the racket no farther back than your shoulder and stroke through the shot so that you have the feeling of the racket strings gliding under the ball. It's a slow-motion version of the slice, basically. This will impart the underspin that will lift the ball over the net by a safe margin, and at the same time bring it down well within the lines.

This "zone defense" method helps you use your groundstrokes intelligently. The more modest the level of skill among players, the greater the role played by errors in determining who wins points. If you keep the ball in play from the red zone, and rarely miss a ball when you're in the caution zone. you're going to win a lot of

63

points thanks to the other guy's mistakes. The opponent will overplay shots long, wide, or into the net, or he will send back balls that land in your "go-zone," and against which you can use the strokes you have practiced.

Part III Fundamentals of Serving

Building the Serve

I put groundstrokes first in order of importance in the process of learning to play tennis but, realistically, a serve should be acquired at about the same time or you won't be able to go out and enjoy practice or play. Most newcomers to tennis want to start competing as soon as possible, and there's nothing wrong with that.

Don't tackle the full serve, however, until:

1. you've absorbed the fundamentals of serving explained in this section,

2. you are secure and comfortable in holding the racket in both grips, and

3. you have hit enough shots off the bounce to have a pretty good sense of how the ball reacts to your racket strings when you hit it.

By attempting too much too soon with the serve, you may form bad habits that'll be hard to shake later on. The serve is a frustrating stroke, both to teach and to learn, and much of the theory about it seems to be obscure and misleading. That's why there are more bad serves in tennis than there are bad forehands, backhands, volleys, or lobs, as a matter of fact. Yet a good serve can lift your game tremendously. If you're a "C" player in every other department, but have an "A" player's serve, you'll beat the "B" player every time. So it's worth the blood, sweat, and tears it takes to get it right.

If you're still working your way toward reasonable consistency in groundstrokes, then, don't rush into serving full tilt. Instead, to enjoy games, use this method of putting the ball into play:

Hold the racket in your *forehand* grip. Stand at the baseline facing the net. Prop the racket on your right shoulder. With your free hand outstretched, lift the ball in the air no more than 18 inches higher than eye level. Then simply slap the ball toward the target court with your racket face flat, or open. Make no effort to hit the ball extra hard, or to guide it to any particular spot in the service box, or to put heavy English on the thing. Just get it in.

Once you're ready to get beyond this level of simply putting the ball in play, it's time to develop the full service motion—a stroke complete with backswing, forward swing, and finish—just like the

67

CORRECT GRIP MAKES IT
EASIER TO SERVE WITH SPIN

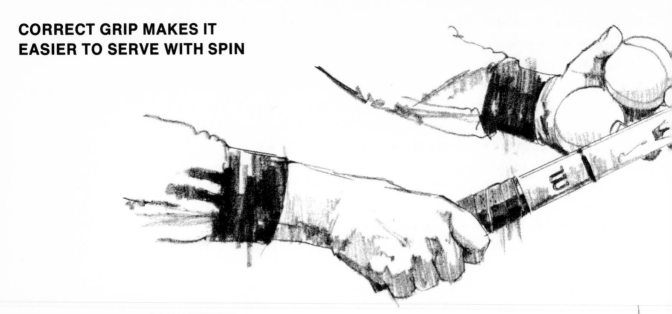

Beginners should hold the racket in the forehand grip when they first start serving, but in time all players should learn to serve with a backhand-type grip (lower left) because that grip makes it possible to develop the brushing action that puts a lot of spin on the ball.

The condensed version of this grip, the "hammer grip" (lower right), is worth trying as you become more advanced, because it permits greater wrist action and, with that, access to greater racket-head speed and also more potential for fooling opponents with serves into unexpected corners.

groundstrokes, to produce serves that mean business, balls that cause some disadvantage for your opponent by landing with depth, pace, and consistency in the service box.

The principal mechanical elements of the serve to be mastered through practice are:

- Controlling the racket with a modified backhand grip instead of forehand grip to promote better wrist action.
- Assuming a balanced stance that points you toward the service box you're aiming for.
- Placing the ball in the air correctly and consistently.
- Coordinating the ball toss and the windup.
- Timing the wrist snap on the forward swing so that the racket strings meet the ball just as it begins to drop.
- Developing the transfer of weight from the back foot as you swing to the front foot at the moment of impact so as to generate pace on the ball for greater depth.

In first practicing the serve, you shouldn't worry about accuracy. Use the entire left or right side of the court as your target area rather than the more elusive confines of the service boxes. This will encourage you to build a relaxed toss and a nice, fluid service motion. It's better to hit your early serves firmly and too long than to hit them feebly and into the net.

As you gain more confidence in the stroking motion, put targets within the service box—ball cans or racket covers will do—and develop accuracy through trial and error. Observe the trajectory of every serve you hit—the shape of its flight, how many feet it clears the net by, and exactly where it lands on the other side. Whenever you hit a good serve, tell yourself "PRINT IT!"—as movie directors holler after a successful take—to ingrain the feeling of the correct stroke in your muscle memory. Try to repeat the shot. When something goes wrong, check your fundamentals for the cause—especially that ball toss. If you know why you did something wrong, you won't get discouraged easily.

How the Serving Stroke Differs from Ground-strokes

A good service motion may be described as a stroke that repeatedly delivers the racket to the ball where you have placed it up in the air, in a manner that gives the resultant shot the distance and height it needs to clear the net, and the speed and direction it requires to force a mistake or a defensive return by the opponent.

The serve is like a forehand or a backhand in that it requires spin on the ball for control and a good weight transfer for power, or pace. But it differs from groundstrokes in three other respects, and that is why it must be approached somewhat on its own terms.

1. The arm motion is different. The serve is like a baseball pitcher's motion to the plate—the arm winds up behind the body and then hurls the ball (or racket) over the head and forward, all in a distinct vertical plane. The forehand, by contrast, is like a third baseman's *sidearm* throw to first base—the arm swings around the body in a horizontal plane. Unless you've been a pitcher or have experience in throwing in some other activity, the serving motion may be a brand-new feeling for you.

2. The wrist, which must be kept firm throughout forehands and backhands, must be allowed its freedom in the service motion, in order to produce the spin needed to control the ball and still hit it reasonably hard. More sidespin/topspin ball rotation is required because the serve has to be brought down into the court in a target area that is half as deep as that for the normal forehand or backhand.

Well-timed wrist action on the forward swing increases what Vic Braden calls the "bite" of the racket strings on the ball—and so increases the rate of rotation of the ball. In effect, it harnesses the energy that a good weight transfer gets into your serve. Many people think that the wrist snap is the source of all power on the serve, but that's false. It slaps on some of the speed, but its main role is to control the ball and keep your main source of power—your transfer of weight—from running amok. The bite is what you feel when you hit with good spin.

The extra wrist action is there for the asking, by serving with a backhand-type grip. I modified my backhand grip by wrapping my thumb around the handle and got even more wrist action. The grip

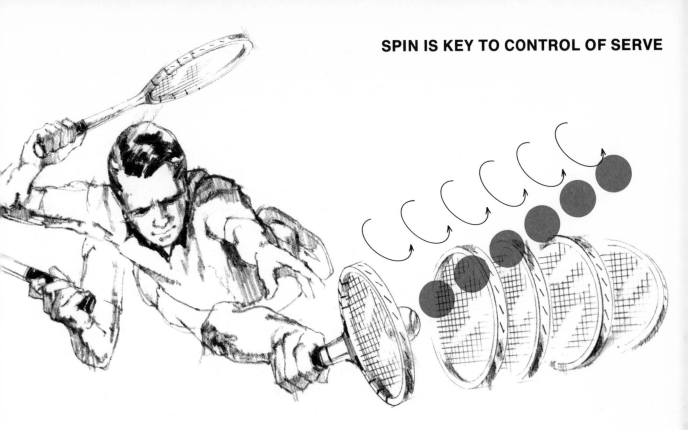

As with groundstrokes, all serves must carry some degree of spin or they won't land within the service box and still carry reasonable speed.

The stroke used for serving must be practiced as a fluid, continuous motion, but it is the interval of impact that governs the type and degree of spin that is imparted to the ball. The money serve for the vast majority of players is the slice serve depicted here, in which the racket strings brush up and around the ball and produce a combination of sidespin and overspin on the shot. This serve should clear the net by a comfortable 3′ or more and follow a curving downward path into the service box. It's vital to swing the racket head through the ball, as shown, and not consciously to try to manipulate the hitting action, or to put 'English' on it. The position of the ball in the air when it is struck, and the path of the racket head itself, are the factors that govern spin. Only advanced players have the skill and experience to vary their serves without substantially changing their toss, by using slightly different hand action during the hit.

that resulted was similar to one you would use for holding a hammer—or throwing a tomahawk. The position of the V between thumb and forefinger is the same as it would be for the backhand grip. The only difference is that the thumb encircles the handle, permitting marginally greater wrist action.

Few players can hit the ball with a sharp glancing blow on the serve from a forehand grip, by the way. I saw Dinny Pails and my longtime doubles partner, Ted Schroeder, do it, but they had the strength and experience to overcome the mechanical hazards inherent in such a serve. It's much easier to get the wrist action you need by gripping the racket backhand style.

3. Another obvious difference: You initiate the action yourself in serving, on the serve, by putting the ball into the air to be stroked, rather than responding to a ball that your opponent has hit, from a stance of your own choosing. Moving to the ball quickly and correctly, so essential to groundstrokes, is irrelevant in serving. That said, it must be pointed out at once that tossing correctly is probably just as hard as setting up for groundstrokes—and it's even more crucial to the success of the resulting shot. You may get to a forehand late and way out of position and still get the ball back. But if the toss isn't in the right place at the right time on your serve, a good arm swing isn't going to compensate as successfully as often.

The fact that you are putting the ball into play from a standstill adds a psychological problem to the physical one. Nervousness, doubt, fear, anxiety, distraction—any of these feelings can enter your mind as you get ready to serve, and sabotage your effort to coordinate the toss of the ball with the windup and forward swing. Negative emotions have less chance to surface during groundstrokes because you're usually in motion and preoccupied with the physical challenge of each shot. When you're moving around, your muscles tend to control your nerves. But when you're at a standstill, your nerves tend to control your muscles.

That's why a relaxed approach is essential in learning the serve and also later in executing it consistently in matches. A relaxed approach will make it much easier for you to establish a tempo in which to coordinate the ball toss, arm swing, release of the wrist, and weight transfer. In this respect, learning to serve well is very much like mastering the full swing in golf. And it has similar tactical value. It's the drive that gets you started right in that game. If you can hold your own serve, you'll have to invent ways to lose in tennis.

There are three basic types of serve—*slice, twist,* and *flat.* They derive their names from the manner in which the racket moves through the ball at impact, and from the type of ball spin, or rotation, that results. It is important to note that the service motion itself is not radically different for each of these types of serve. *The placement of the ball on the toss invites varying racket action during the interval of impact and is the main determining factor in the type of serve that is produced.* Ellsworth Vines and Pancho Gonzales are the only players I've ever watched who could hit all three types of serve off nearly the same toss. In any case, the serving fundamentals which follow apply to any type of serve.

For the *slice,* the ball is tossed in front and to the right. The racket swings outward but the strings bite through the ball on an up-and-around path, imparting a combination of topspin and sidespin and producing a curving trajectory in the flight of the shot. Characteristically, a good slice serve clears the net by 2 to 2½ feet. Upon landing, it bounces to the left (off a right-handed serve), or, in the direction of the prevailing rotation, the sidespin.

(Note that the slice serve has nothing in common with the underspin backhand, which is also often referred to as a slice. The slice serve is hit with sidespin/topspin. The slice backhand is hit with underspin.)

For the *twist,* the ball is tossed directly over the head. The racket comes from an angle more *below* the ball and so imparts more topspin than sidespin. A combination of both spins, but just the reverse of the slice in where the emphasis lies. A good twist serve

Why the Slice Serve Pays Off

73

travels in a higher, more looping trajectory, clearing the net by 3 to 3½ feet and dropping more sharply into the service box than the slice does. This time it bounces, or kicks, to the *right*—once again in the direction of the dominant or prevailing spin.

A good *flat* serve is not hit entirely without spin, as the name implies, for it must have some topspin on it to make the ball descend into the service box. It has more spin—and much more speed—than the beginner's get-it-into-play flat serve. But it doesn't have as much spin as the slice or the twist, and it rarely clears the net by more than one foot without going long.

For that serve, the ball is tossed over the forward shoulder, causing the racket to swing up more directly from the ball, with much less of a spin-producing bite.

In general, the slice can be used to attack an opponent's backhand in both the first and second courts. (The first court is the forehand or right court; the second court is the backhand or left court.) It can be used effectively to pull the opponent out of the court in the first court. With somewhat less spin and more pace, it can also be hit down the middle into both courts for the occasional ace-by-surprise.

Mechanically, the slice is superior to the twist because it involves a more natural throwing motion that puts less strain on the physique. The twist forces you to take the racket back with more pressure on the hitting arm. It also requires an arching back bend— to set the racket in position on the windup to hit more up on the ball—so it's tough on players with weak backs or without the supple muscles of youth.

Another minor mechanical advantage of the slice is that the ball toss does not have to be so high, so it can be developed with more consistency. The ball has to be spotted 6 to 8 inches higher for an extreme twist, to give the racket a shot at its underside.

In terms of tactics, the slice serve tends to land deeper in the service box than the more sharply dropping twist, so it prevents more opponents from attacking off the return.

Also, the slice carries on a more shallow pitch, after it has bounced, than the twist serve does, adding to its effective depth and making the receiver get down lower. True, a good twist produces a high-bouncing ball that can be quite effective into a receiver's backhand. But it's a serve that many alert opponents will learn to move in on and take on the rise. The steeper pitch of the bounce simply makes it more vulnerable to attack.

The slice beats the all-out flat serve on several counts as well.

Mechanically, the slice is much easier to execute. You can get bite on a slice reasonably well if your timing or toss is slightly off, but a flat serve must be timed more precisely.

Tactically, the slice is more reliable. A flat serve clears the net by inches, so there is more danger of hitting into the net, and it is struck with less controlling spin, so there is more danger of hitting long. The average player can learn to get a good slice on his first serve 70 to 80 percent of the time. Even if you practiced a hard, flat serve religiously, you would not be likely to get it 30 to 40 percent of the time on first serves. That would leave you stuck with a slow version of the flat for your second try—a pattycake shot that of all serves is the easiest to attack—or a spin-type serve that you haven't really practiced enough to get in consistently. And knowledge that your second serve isn't all that much will make it even harder to get the first one in, and so numerous points will be literally thrown away on double-faults or sitting ducks.

Even at the highest level, the flat serve is not a money shot. On the pro circuit today, particularly as emphasis on the return of serve has increased, and as ultrafast surfaces such as grass have lost prominence, most players now hit first serves at a three-quarter pace, rather than going for aces. The 1975 Wimbledon final between Arthur Ashe and Jimmy Connors was a good example of this change in emphasis. Ashe chose to shelve his cannonball serve out of respect for Connors's great returning ability. Instead, he attacked Connors with his excellent wide slice serve—and largely beat him thanks to the superb control he had on that serve that day.

Serving Accuracy Starts in the Stance

The rules say that you have to stand somewhere to the right of the midpoint of the baseline when you are serving to the left service box, and somewhere to the left of the midpoint when you are serving to the right service box.

No rule governs *where* along that line you must stand, so long as it is between midpoint and sideline, but, for singles, most players assume a stance between ½ to 1½ feet from the centerline in the first court and from 1½ to 2½ feet from the centerline in the second court. Stick to this positioning range yourself in learning the serve.

Serving from an extra-wide position in either court is not usually desirable because it leaves one side of your court unprotected.

The slightly wider position in the second court permits you to face a slightly lower part of the net. Later on, you'll also find that you get more returns back down the center of the court when you serve from the wider position in the second court. So you'll have an extra yard in which to use the forehand on your second shot.

Incidentally, there's no rule preventing you from standing at a distance *behind* the baseline, but that effectively adds height to the net (you're not allowed to run up to the line and then serve), so it is nearly universal that servers also locate themselves as close to the baseline as they can, just as, for most singles play, they stand as near the midpoint line as we've indicated. One of the finest present-day servers, Arthur Ashe, happens to stand 8 to 10 inches or so behind the line to avoid foot-faulting—you're not allowed to cross the baseline with either foot until after you've hit the ball. Arthur has the habit of sliding forward with his front foot as he tosses the ball, and if he did not start farther back, he would slide across the line before making contact. This is an idiosyncrasy that Ashe himself would not recommend to anyone starting in the game.

I was fanatical about planting the front foot exactly where I wanted it to be when I would pivot on it, and I made it a constant in my service stance. I could put it a hair from the baseline without fear of foot-faulting (only one fault was ever called against me) because I knew it never fidgeted. I think it would be important for most players to try to achieve the same stability.

EADY TO SERVE

e main figures here show the best positions in
nich to stand to attack an opponent's backhand
th your slice serve in the first and second courts.
anding farther away from center in the second
urt makes it easier to angle your slice into the
ckhand corner and still cross the net where it
lower.

By standing almost dead center on the base-
e in the first court, you can pick on a very
eak backhand by serving down the middle.
Note variations for attacking the backhand
a left-handed opponent.

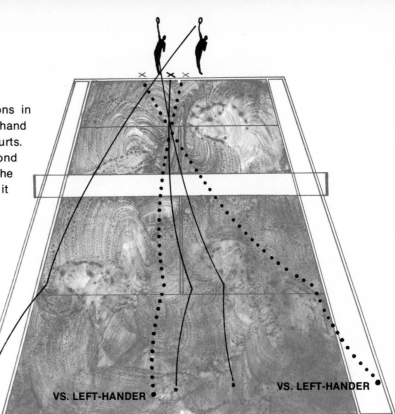

VS. LEFT-HANDER

VS. LEFT-HANDER

VS. LEFT-HANDER

VS. LEFT-HANDER

The feet must be aligned in a way that makes it natural to swing in the direction of the target court, and ultimately to transfer your weight in that direction during the stroke. It is considerably easier to learn the service motion without the weight shift, so, for now, keep the weight on the front foot when serving. Spread your feet comfortably apart—just as you would do in a good ready position for groundstrokes. They should be about shoulder width apart, with the back foot parallel to the baseline, and with the front foot pointing in. *An arrow through your heels or hips would point directly at the service box you're aiming for.*

To make this alignment consistent for both courts, there must be a variation in the position of the front foot. In the first court, the front foot should be placed at about 45 degrees to the baseline. That sets your heels and hips on the line pointing to the target court. In the second court, the front foot must be placed at less of an angle to the baseline—15 to 20 degrees for most players—in order to maintain the same relation of hips to the target court.

Toss with Touch for Consistency

The ability to place the ball consistently to the spot where you can hit it effectively is the single most important ingredient in developing a good service motion. A consistent toss helps you to automate your service motion just as meeting balls off the bounce in the same strike zone helps you to groove your groundstrokes. If you toss the ball to five or six different spots in the air, you'll need five or six different swings to chase after it, and that will hardly produce uniform results.

The trick is to coordinate the action of the hand lifting the ball with the action of the hand drawing the racket back. If this is done well, the two reactions—ball rising to a peak after it is released, and racket head swinging forward to meet the ball—are likely to mesh as well. You must be able to meet the ball at or just below its peak, because that's when it's almost motionless, and so an easier target.

If you meet the ball on the way up, you'll tend to hit long. If you hit it on the way down, you'll probably serve into the net.

It's a package deal, so after you've obtained a clear picture of how the separate parts of the service motion function and have familiarized yourself with them individually, put them together and practice them that way.

For an effective slice, and assuming you're in the stance we've just described, the ball should be released slightly in front of you to your right, with your tossing arm finishing in a Statue of Liberty attitude, or about 30 degrees from perpendicular.

The distance of the toss from your body should be about half a racket length, or 1 to 1½ feet, as measured from your forward foot along a line that points out toward your target. Practice the toss in your correct stance at the service line. Let the ball drop, mark the spot where it lands, and check its distance from your body.

The *height* of the toss, again for the slice, should be about 3 feet over your head. Mark this distance on some tall fence and practice lifting balls into the air to that spot, then bring your sense of that special spatial relation over to the service line and put it to work there.

Both figures are approximate because important individual factors must also be taken into account.

The exact distance of the toss from your body depends in part on the length of your arms and the fullness of your motion. The more weight transfer you develop on the serve, the more room you'll need to operate.

The exact height of the toss depends in part on your natural rhythm. A slower windup would dictate a higher toss, a fast one a lower toss.

Once you've found your natural range, the idea is to mass-produce your tosses so they're never more than a couple of inches off the mark. Minor variations in toss are inevitable and, in a sense, welcome in that they yield variations in the serve itself and so complicate your attack for the opponent. Major variations—of six inches or more—prevent you from ever developing a consistent motion.

TOSS TO STRETCH YOUR POTENTIAL

It's impossible to groove your serve until you learn to the ball in the air consistently—to the same height an tance from your body, in order to be able to swing full not so that you must over-reach and lose your balance toss for the slice serve is depicted here with the aid racket that has been placed on the court surface at angle from the baseline. If a correctly placed ball we lowed to drop from the peak of its toss, instead of hit, it would bounce on that racket. Use a spare racket ilarly to help you standardize your own ball toss—and to encourage you to step into the court with the back on the finish.

You'll find that if the ball is tossed too near your body, your swing will feel cramped and you won't be able to snap the wrist and release the racket fully. If it is too far away from you—toward the sideline or toward the fence behind you—you'll tend to lose your balance as you swing. If it goes up too high, you'll have to wait for it, and if it's too low, you'll have to rush to hit it. Either way your tempo will be spoiled. One important variation in the toss will occur when you are sufficiently advanced in your overall game to want to follow serve into net, at least on occasion. In order to do this effectively, you should toss the ball an extra 3 to 6 inches closer to net, in effect leading yourself into the court.

Hold only one ball at a time when grooving your toss. Bill Tilden used to hold three or four balls in his hand prior to serving, but that was for showmanship—and he had bigger hands than most players. Holding one ball not only makes it easier to lift the ball gently, and with control, but it leaves your hand free to help with the racket and the grip change, if required, after you serve.

Try to release the ball at shoulder level, or even slightly higher, if it's comfortable to do so, and make this point of release a consistent feature of your toss. That aids consistency by reducing the time spent by the ball in the air on its own.

If the toss looks bad, don't swing at it. Let the ball drop and start all over again. Taking pot shots at errant tosses not only impedes your efforts to groove a uniform toss, but it exposes you to the risk of strain to your wrist, elbow, shoulder, and even your back.

Packaging the Parts of the Stroke

Finally, the ball toss, windup, and forward swing must be packaged into one smooth, fluid motion.

In the first half of the motion, the tossing arm lifts the ball in the air, as we've described, and the hitting arm brings the racket back into hitting position.

The exact path the racket takes on the windup may vary according to individuals. Some players start the racket back around the body—just as they might do in preparing to hit a forehand. Others —myself among them—prefer to let the racket head drop straight down and then swing back up behind the body in a pendulum motion. Still other players lift the racket up in a direct, almost abrupt manner to place it in the hitting slot—Pancho Gonzales had such a windup.

The hitting position itself—the end result of those different windups—does not vary substantially among good players. The elbow is raised so that the upper arm is parallel to the ground. The forearm is folded all the way back on the upper arm. The hand holding the racket is behind the head. The grip on the racket handle is firm. There is no particular strain or awkwardness felt anywhere. It is as comfortable as the windup position for throwing a ball—which in fact it closely resembles, and with reason, for the forward swing of the arm is essentially a throwing motion.

Practice the first half of the service motion so that the hand holding the racket completes its windup as the ball lifts free of the other hand now outstretched in its toss. There's a natural correlation between the two actions and it is easy to come by.

In the second half of the service motion, the tossing arm falls away and the hitting arm, as though hurling a ball, propels the racket forward.

Practice the second half of the service motion so that the racket meets the ball immediately upon the start of the ball's descent from the peak of its toss. This is when the ball will be virtually motionless and therefore easiest to target upon.

The hitting arm should feel extended at impact, but not stretched to the point of stiffness or so as to jeopardize balance.

The bite of racket strings on ball should be solid. Don't try to manipulate the racket in any way to slice the ball, or "cut around it." Remember that the initial direction of the racket on the forward swing is outward, and not until after the ball is hit and on its way do the hitting arm and racket swing down across the front of the server. Trust in your backhand grip, well-timed wrist action, and the correct positioning of the ball in the toss to make it possible for the spin-producing racket action to occur.

82

A good weight transfer is the last thing you should try to develop in your service motion. Last but not least—for a proper and well-timed transfer adds pace to the serve just as it does to groundstrokes. And a serve with pace lands deeper in the service box and acquires more depth by virtue of its harder, faster bounce. If you're consistently deep on your serves, your opponent will have to stand deeper to return, all but removing the chance for him to hit out on returns.

The degree of skill of your opponent determines how deep you must place the ball in order to hold your serve. If the opponent poops back everything, you might be able to place serves 6 to 7 feet inside his service line and still win. But we're assuming you're going to face tougher opponents. To keep good players pinned to their baseline, you must learn to put a fast serve 30 inches or less inside their service line. The only way to do that consistently is by learning to use your body weight in your service motion.

The weight transfer helps in other ways besides giving depth. It helps make the service motion fluid and continuous, a "one-piece swing" without hitches, hiccups, or pregnant pauses. It protects you better from the risk of injury. There's less effort or strain on the arm and shoulder when you come through with your weight. It also protects you from fatigue. In his playing days Gonzales would be hitting serves as hard in the fifth set as he was in the first, because he let his weight shift do all the work.

The weight transfer improves your chances of timing the serve well. It lengthens the service motion, giving more latitude for well-timed hits on days when your timing is off, or on crucial points when there is a tendency for the muscles to freeze up. Players without an effective weight transfer tend to double-fault or hit too short. Their serves rely too much on abbreviated arm motions and go haywire under pressure or when attempting to play extra safe. When you transfer your weight properly, you're apt to serve the ball deeply in spite of your nerves.

I probably had the most conspicuous weight shift in the game, then or now. I actually stepped back with the rear foot in my

Weight Transfer, Pace, Depth

83

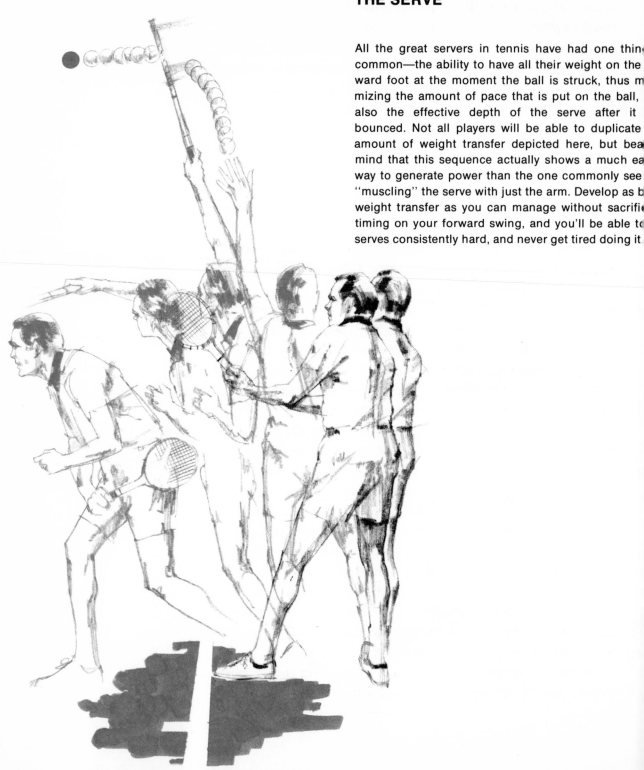

WEIGHT TRANSFER = PACE ON THE SERVE

All the great servers in tennis have had one thing common—the ability to have all their weight on the ward foot at the moment the ball is struck, thus m mizing the amount of pace that is put on the ball, also the effective depth of the serve after it bounced. Not all players will be able to duplicate amount of weight transfer depicted here, but bea mind that this sequence actually shows a much ea way to generate power than the one commonly see "muscling" the serve with just the arm. Develop as b weight transfer as you can manage without sacrifi timing on your forward swing, and you'll be able to serves consistently hard, and never get tired doing it serving stance, and then let all the weight roll onto the front foot with my forward swing. I felt I was getting all the help I could from my body that way. My service motion resembled that of an out-fielder rearing back to throw someone out at home—as opposed, say, to the motion of a second baseman getting rid of the ball for a double play. In other words, there was nothing cramped or tenta-tive about my motion.

Of the pros who have come to prominence since my time, John Newcombe came closest to using his weight as I always tried to use mine on the serve. The great depth Newcombe obtained on both first and second serves when he was in his prime made him the premier server of the day. It may be attributed to his fine transfer.

I wouldn't offer the stepping-back method as a model for gen-erating the weight transfer because I think too many players would have trouble keeping the ball toss and forward swing in sync. How-ever, the principle of adding pace to your serve by means of the controlled weight transfer is sound, and you definitely should try to incorporate it into your service motion.

The simplest and most effective way to transfer weight is by shifting the hips. That is where most of your body weight is, any-way—in and around the area of your hips. If you're in a good balanced stance at the outset of the service motion, you're set up to use your weight effectively. The bulk of the weight is on your forward foot, which is planted, and your left hip is looking in the direction you want to hit the ball. Shift the hips back on the windup and the bulk of your weight will be on the back foot. Shift the hips forward on the forward swing, and the bulk of the weight will move to your front foot. Throughout, the front hip remains on line with your target area.

In striving for the full weight transfer, guard against hopping, leaping, or lunging at the ball. If your weight isn't on the front foot at the moment you hit the ball, the transfer won't take place. Remember, all the really great servers in tennis history kept the front foot anchored at impact.

After impact, the momentum generated by the weight transfer

will naturally carry you forward. The back foot will pivot around the anchored front foot and step across the baseline into the court and in the direction of the serve itself. The racket-head speed generated by proper wrist action will cause your hitting arm and racket to swing around your body, with the racket itself pointing down at the court. Gonzales would actually hit the court surface on the followthrough—you would hear the click of his racket as you got your own racket back to return.

Percentage Tactics on the Serve

I would sum up serving tactics as follows:

Get the first serve in.
Get the serve in deep.

The probability of your first serve going in forces the receiver to guard both his forehand and backhand sides. The probability of it landing deep makes him stand back, at or behind the baseline. A deep first serve, then, is really a ball that anchors the opponent in his red-light zone—and stops him from attacking on the return. Serve eight feet shorter and, instead of standing two feet behind his baseline, your opponent can stand six feet *inside* the line.

You literally cede territory to the other side when you miss the first serve. The opponent not only moves in, he also shades the court slightly to favor hitting his stronger shot, usually the forehand. And if he's reasonably quick, you can depend on him to try to run around the second serve to attack it with the forehand.

A high first-serve percentage depends entirely on the type of serve you are trying to hit. Our rationale for developing a slice serve, explained earlier, is that it yields this high percentage. Even a top player would be lucky to hit 40 percent going all out for aces —service winners hit so hard that the opponent can't get his racket on them. That's why half the participants in those fast-serve contests are lucky to get one good serve from their five or six tries. Speed kills.

The slice serve can also consistently produce the depth necessary to keep the receiver in his red zone after the ball lands. Any player willing to put in the practice time can learn to slice his serves to within three feet of the service line.

A flat serve is slowed by clay. A twist sits up on concrete and many indoor surfaces. *A deep serve is a deep serve on any surface.*

Depth on the second serve, which is most easily obtained by having a good basic slice serve, makes up for lapses on the first serve. My own second serve got me over the hump in many matches, because it consistently hit within eighteen inches or closer to the service line. Can you appreciate the psychological value of having a dependably deep second serve? I know it always gave me more confidence in approaching my first serve in tight spots. I never had to say to myself, "Oh, God, it's 30–40 and I've *got* to get this in!"

Billie Jean King's deep second serve bolstered her serving under pressure, certainly. By contrast, Margaret Court, with possibly the strongest first serve of any woman player in history, tended to waver under pressure—because her second serve wasn't much, and she knew it.

The same works for ordinary players, only more so. Forget about aces. Master the slice so that you can get the first serve in eight out of ten times, and so that when you do face a second serve, you can use the same spin with confidence.

ATTACK THE OPPONENT'S WEAKER STROKE

The slice can be hit anywhere in either service box. If the opponent's backhand is decidedly weaker than his forehand, you should serve to his backhand nine out of ten times. If he is going to make errors consistently for you or produce weak returns with the backhand, don't tempt his forehand just for the sake of variety. Keep him honest—but only on unimportant points.

The aiming adjustment required in slicing serves into the backhand varies for each court. It's a matter of judgment and feel, and of decisively projecting where and how you want the serve to fly in your mind as you stand prior to tossing the ball.

In the first court, a good slice crosses the net 18 inches to 2 feet

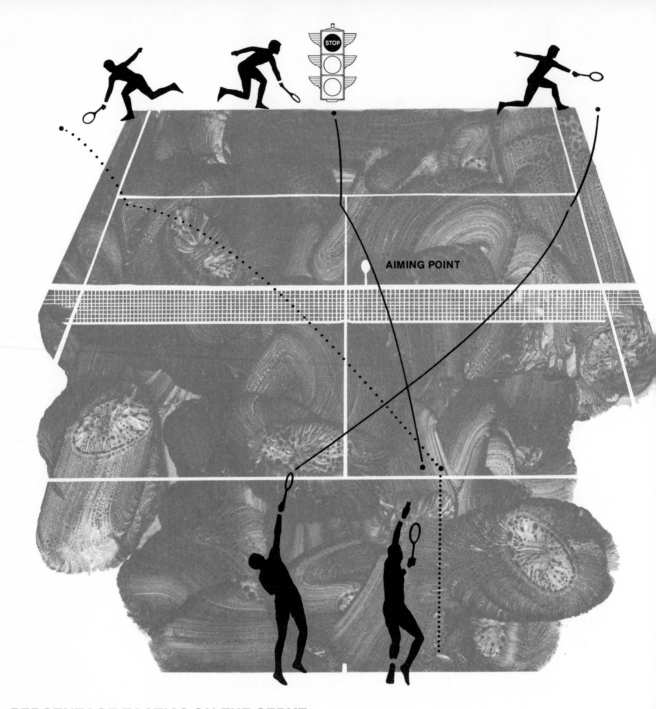

AIMING POINT

PERCENTAGE TACTICS ON THE SERVE

The slice serve can be used to hit any corner in either service box, but it does the most damage when it is hit into the opponent's backhand. If it lands within 2 to 3′ of the service line, it will bounce deep enough to keep the receiver firmly in his STOP or RED-LIGHT ZONE, thus forcing a defensive return.

A bonus for learning a good slice serve is the variation available to you in the first court. By tossing the ball a few inches more toward the sideline, as shown, you can produce a wide serve to pull the opponent off the court—another STOP ZONE position—or, should it catch him by surprise, you could score a service winner.

to the *right* of center, and then curves into the backhand corner, so you really have to "aim" into the second court.

When you're serving into the second court, the angle is different and you must put more spin on the ball to make sure it gets into the backhand corner. The hips are more closed in the stance, and the ball toss is slightly closer to the over-the-head position of the ball for the twist-type serve.

You won't force the opponent wide with your slice to the second court, but if you slice his return back in the same direction and as deep as possible, you'll have him in trouble. If his backhand is really weak, his next shot will probably land short near your service line—if it gets over at all.

Every server has a favorite court and you'll find that you feel more enjoyment and confidence in serving from one side than from the other. That just means you should pay more attention to your second shot when you're serving to your second-best court.

If an opponent is equally good—or equally bad—from both sides, serve wide to him in both courts to make him move. In the first court, you'll be serving wide to his forehand; in the second court, wide to his backhand. In each case you force him to run off the court to return, then run back to recover the center. The extra footwork forces mistakes.

SERVE WIDE TO AN OPPONENT WHOSE FOREHAND AND BACKHAND ARE EQUAL

Just as a baseball pitcher might use curves or changeups to make his bread-and-butter fastball more effective, it's important to mix up serves in tennis to prevent an opponent from anticipating and eventually improving through sheer repetition the weaker stroke you've been attacking. This is called keeping him honest, but what you are really doing is keeping him *tentative*. Hitting just a few serves to his forehand in the course of a match evens out your attack in his mind and prevents him from focusing on just his backhand side.

Serve to the strong side when the opponent has moved over so much to protect his weak side that there is an opening big enough for you to go for the ace without altering your normal serve.

PICK YOUR SPOTS TO SERVE TO THE STRONG SIDE

89

Serve to the forehand in the first court to really open up the court to attack a weak backhand on the next shot.

Or serve to the strong side when you're ahead 40–love or 40–15—when you can afford to lose a point.

SERVE INTO THE BODY FOR CHANGE OF PACE AND TO EXPLOIT SLOWPOKES

You can jam an opponent if you aim your slice to bounce up into the body on his backhand side. As he moves sideways to give himself room to stroke, the ball moves with him because of its slice spin. The same shot into the forehand side is not effective because it doesn't chase the receiver.

Big, slow-footed players usually have a hard time getting out of their own way; against such opponents the slice into the body might be used as much as the serve directly into the weakness.

SERVE TO ELICIT A RETURN TO YOUR FOREHAND

To get your power forehand into play immediately after serving, slice the ball wide to the opponent's forehand in the first court. Very few players can return such a serve down the line. Most have to pull it crosscourt, and that allows you to use your forehand. Serving down the middle to the opponent's forehand in the second court forces returns back down the middle, so again you can use the forehand on the second shot.

This tactic wouldn't work if your slice wasn't wide enough in the first court or deep enough in the second court to force the player to make a defensive return. It might not work if your opponent's forehand is really strong.

In those two cases you're better off sticking to attacking the backhand on the serve and also off his return. If you attacked his strong forehand off the return, he might pull you crosscourt with it. You won't want to hit it to his backhand because, even though it's his weaker stroke, he's got an open court behind you to hit to. So you'd have to hit it crosscourt to his strength again. Moral: Keep it on his backhand until he makes a mistake or gives you a short ball.

For every game you serve in singles, you're also going to play a game in which you receive serve. To the extent that your opponent can put the ball into play where and how he likes off the serve, he holds the upper hand. However, if you make the server work hard for his points by committing as few mistakes as possible, your chances of eroding his confidence, forcing mistakes by him, and eventually breaking serve will be greater.

Many players try to do too much on their returns, however. Unless you're playing someone with an awful serve, or someone who rushes the net all the time, you should seldom hit for winners off the return. The idea is to protect your capital, not to blow it.

Anticipation can be your greatest ally on the return, so develop in your waiting position the attributes that encourage you to remain alert, watchful, and ready to spring into action.

I find that a wide stance, with feet slightly farther apart than shoulder width, and pointing outward—like a duck's feet—helps to get you off the mark quickly to the left or the right depending on the direction of the serve. It also helps you reach a bit farther if there isn't time to step.

Don Budge—probably the greatest receiver of all time in the game—had an exceptionally wide stance, and with his extraordinary anticipation, he was also able to stand in close. In matches with him, I always had the feeling I was serving to a dragon who would gobble up just about anything I sent over.

Keep weight more on the toes than on the heels in this stance, and keep your knees comfortably flexed. Hold the racket in front of you, with your free hand at its throat, equally prepared for forehand or backhand.

Hold the racket high in front of you, not at waist level or to one side, awaiting serve, and always start in the forehand grip. Remember, the forehand requires more preparation than the backhand, so if you're in the grip for that stroke at the start, you'll be that much ahead. The pivot into the backhand backswing can be made much more quickly, especially if you use the free hand to get the racket started back.

Returning Serves

PREPARATION

PERCENTAGE TACTICS ON RETURN OF SERVE

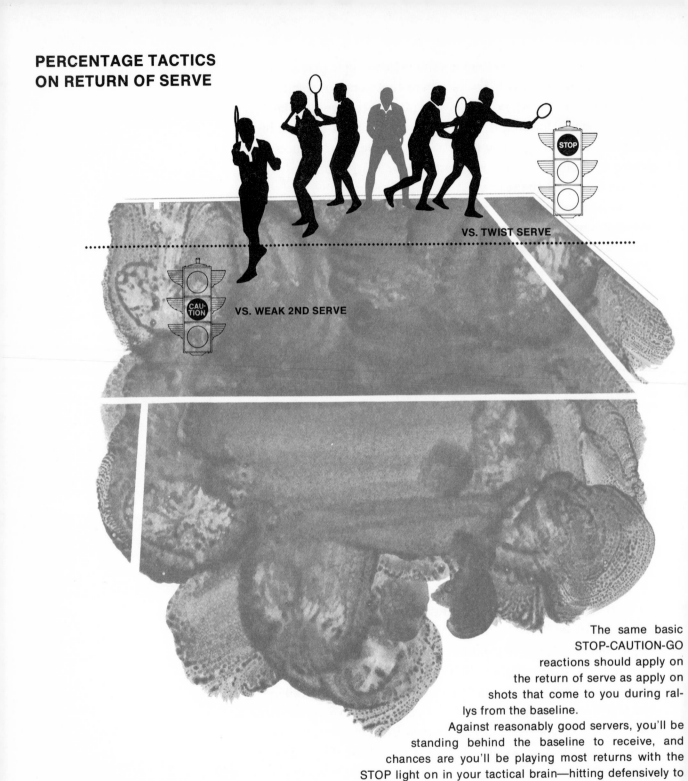

VS. TWIST SERVE

VS. WEAK 2ND SERVE

The same basic STOP-CAUTION-GO reactions should apply on the return of serve as apply on shots that come to you during rallys from the baseline.

Against reasonably good servers, you'll be standing behind the baseline to receive, and chances are you'll be playing most returns with the STOP light on in your tactical brain—hitting defensively to make sure you get the ball back over the net and in play.

Against the twist serve or weak second serve, both of which are depicted being returned here, you should stand *inside* the baseline, however. The twist serve tends to kick towards the sideline (in the second court) and if you are too far back, you'll have to run off the court to return it, leaving a big angle for your opponent to exploit.

The depth of the serve determines the position you have to take up in attempting the return, and that position tips you off to your realistic options, just as it does during exchanges of groundstrokes.

If the serve forces you to take the ball in your red-light zone, forget any thoughts of winning the point for now. Don't even worry about *where* on the other side you should put the return—just be sure you don't miss it.

If the serve comes to you in your caution zone, you should be able to set up in time to control the *direction* of your return better. So try to play these returns to the opponent's backhand, hoping for a weaker shot or an error.

If the serve reaches you in your green-light zone, you not only have time to set up and thus direct the shot, but also to run around, if necessary, to take the shot on your stronger forehand side and pack more pace into it. When this opportunity arises, hit the ball hard and to the opponent's open corner for a forcing shot and maybe a placement—an outright winner. Even if the open corner happens to be on the opponent's forehand side, smack it there.

Make a special effort to run around short balls in the first court, because that brings you into the center, in better position to cover the next shot. In this case, you'd hit the ball down the line to the open corner, which also happens to be the opponent's backhand side. Double trouble for him.

The side to which the serve comes also influences the type of return you can play effectively.

If the serve comes to your backhand (as it usually will if your opponent has heard anything at all about tennis tactics), take the attitude that you're not going to try to do an awful lot with it. Make a short swing and play it back safely with a nice firm slice to the opponent's backhand. If you can get it into the backhand and deep enough to keep the opponent in his red-light or caution zone, he won't be able to do much to you. If he rushes net on you, hit it to his backhand side, only much shorter.

If the serve comes to your forehand, you're ready for it because you're in your forehand grip, so go for a deep, controlled drive, in

RETURN BACKHANDS
SAFELY,
FOREHANDS HARD

whichever direction makes you feel more comfortable. The depth of your shot will keep the opponent pinned to the baseline. You're not trying to pound a winner, but you're not afraid of it, either.

Where you stand awaiting serve depends on the type of serve that your opponent hits most of the time, and on your own natural quickness.

If the serve of the opponent generally comes in *fast and flat*, stand 2 to 3 feet behind the baseline and shorten your backswing. You don't have time to take a big cut at the ball and get consistent results. But when the ball gets to you fast, you'll be surprised how fast you can get it back with the shorter stroke.

If the serve comes in *short* all the time, stand inside the baseline. The shorter the serve is, the closer in you should stand, to intimidate the server and make him feel terrible about his game.

If your opponent has a good *slice* serve (such as I urge you to try to develop), you should also stand inside the baseline, especially in the first court, so that you can catch the ball before it begins to spin away and pull you off beyond the sideline with it. Once you do stand in against a good slice server, you become more vulnerable down the middle, but it's a risk you have to take. Your opponent has earned the option of going for an ace down the middle on you by developing the good slice.

The slicer won't have you in pincers in the second court, as a rule, however. A slice serve tends to spin toward you in this court, so it can't pull you as wide. You can cover serves to your forehand and backhand equally well.

If the server has a good *twist*, you should stand inside the baseline, especially in the *second* court, so that you can hit the ball before it's had a chance to spin up and carry you out of court with it. Try to nip its spin in the bud by meeting the ball on the way up.

Against an opponent who has mastered the slice *or* the twist, be prepared to do more with your feet on all returns. Shorten up your swing, on both backswing and followthrough, because you would make too many errors trying to take a full swing, while also in motion. And when you are pulled wide, remember to return

94

the ball *crosscourt*, so that you end up in a better court position after making the shot.

As you gain in confidence and strokemaking ability, you can begin to consider taking the initiative more often on the return of serve—depending always on the quality of your opponent and, if you're competing, on your standing in the match.

One tactic is to exploit more fully that weak second serve by following your return off it into net. Hit your forehand down the line or crosscourt, whichever makes you feel more comfortable; but bear in mind that an attack on his backhand is likely to put you in a better volleying position in the court. More often than not, you'll get a setup that you can volley away—even before you've learned to volley.

Another tactic is to go for winners off every ball served to your forehand. This contradicts the more conservative outlook on returns expressed just a few pages ago, but in the hands of a player who has developed an extra-strong forehand, it makes sense. Consider the effect it has on the opponent. Even if you miss some of your attempts to capitalize on the serves hit to your strong side, the server will consciously or unconsciously avoid the forehand when the time comes for him to serve on a crucial point. And if you can depend on the serve coming into your backhand, you'll be better prepared for the big point.

Attack tactic No. 3 is to make your return the first in a combination of shots designed to get your opponent to hit a ball to the place where you can tee off on it. If your best shot is a forehand down the line, for example, the only way you may ever get around to using it is to hit a short backhand down the line first, one that invites the opponent to come in and go for a placement crosscourt —the spot where you want the ball to be in order to uncork your Sunday punch.

Part IV Finding a Workable Style

With the foundations of serving and groundstrokes in place, it is time to evaluate the particular physical and emotional traits that you bring onto the tennis court. No one can master every phase of the game, and a realistic self-appraisal at this stage will help you pinpoint where to place the emphasis in learning more advanced shots and also in refining and improving your basic strokes.

A little later, we'll trace two basic tennis strategies. One is an attack strategy built around a strong serve or approach shot, the volley, and the overhead. The other is a counterattack strategy, built around the passing shot and the lob.

It's important to understand how both these strategies work, even though your personal playing style will largely determine which strategy you can adopt more successfully. Your skill with the shots upon which each strategy are built also must be considered, so that you develop point-winning combinations that truly reflect what you can do.

Size, strength, quickness, mobility, and coordination are the main physical traits that influence the development of a playing style.

If you're a big, slow-moving type, your best chance to become a good player is not to try to become a net-rushing volleyer, but to develop more power from the backcourt immediately. And you can do that—for if you're big, all your strokes are longer and naturally productive of more power. Practice for greater depth and speed on your serve and develop a big shot that you can use on your forehand or even your backhand side for attempted placements. Force yourself to take balls on the rise, not necessarily because you're going to be a great attacking player, but because if you don't, your physical limitations will doom you to being a terrible defensive player. Go for winners in your yellow and even your red zones on the assumption that the longer the point goes on, the less chance you have to win it. Accept the fact that if you don't take a whack at it when you can, there's a good chance the opponent will hit the next one out of your reach.

If you're small in physique, chances are you won't have the kind of power that can force errors or create placements from the base-

Playing Your Own Game

line, no matter how much you devote yourself to work on your serve and groundstrokes. But you're likely to be faster, more agile and better-coordinated than the big fellow, and those are the traits *you* should build on. Develop a running game. If you are quick, you can get away with standing inside the baseline to receive serve, or suckering players into hitting to open corners during rallies, and coming up to net even before you have anything to attack with.

If you're small *and* slow, or lacking in the stamina you need to play a running game, then you have to find another way to win, and that must be through steadiness and concentration. In fact, the hardest style in the world to beat may well be that of the player who'll do nothing to beat himself. So if you're not able to bomb your serve, or move like a racehorse, then spend more time on building a consistent, dependable ground game, and become master of the lob, to use in lieu of passing shots against players who attack you at net, and to keep the ball in play. Junk balls— shots with little or no pace on them—and perhaps drop shots, for surprising players caught behind their baseline, should be part of your repertory. But most of what you are trying to do is to do nothing—buzz around the other player's game with what little you have until he gets so exasperated that he makes the mistakes.

All tactical considerations are rooted in the style of play chosen. If you're only good from the baseline—as many junior or weaker players must content themselves to be—you're going to have to move your opponent around patiently until you finally can pass him with your point-winner. If you're only good inside the service line, you have to keep the ball going somehow until you have the chance to go in.

Off the ball that the big-slow player hits for a placement, the small-fast player moves in on and hits an approach and the small-slow player just hits it back safely, calmly, and deeply, hoping for an error or an even shorter ball on the next shot.

The style chosen must reflect your true capabilities. If Nastase wants someone to serve to his forehand in the first court, he'll stand 4 to 5 feet inside the sideline. He's fast enough to catch up with the serve if the opponent tries to slice it wide. I was never as quick as Nastase, so I could never leave as much real estate open in awaiting serve.

There are two ways to feel good about being a volleyer. One is to have a terrific way of coming to net, either behind a deep serve or a good approach shot. I played that way—behind first and second serves whenever I played on fast courts, and coming in on my forehand slice down the line when I played on slower surfaces.

The other way is to be so fast and agile that you can come in off even a mediocre serve or approach and still cover the range of possible returns by the opponent. Tom Okker and Raul Ramirez are good examples among today's pros of players whose fast reflexes and busybody style make their net games effective.

Don't let vanity or admiration of some other player's style lead you into a false notion of your skills. The most effective competitors are the ones who are unabashedly pragmatic about themselves.

Are You Really a Forehand Player?

In addition to looking at your physical traits candidly, screen your shotmaking abilities. I've suggested that the majority of players will be better off developing an offensive shot off their forehand side and using the backhand strictly for defense. But are you really a forehand player? If your backhand naturally has more zip than your forehand, that's the stroke you should use to do the damage, and rely on forehands only for control.

My friend Vic Braden actually teaches his pupils a backhand grip that sometimes improves the backhand at the expense of the forehand. The hand is positioned a fraction farther behind the racket handle than it is in the conventional backhand grip that I advocate. More precisely, the knuckle of the index finger is positioned on the top right ridge, or edge, of the grip. This puts the bulk of the palm right on top of the handle and promotes an extra solid feel in the backhand grip. In watching players who've adopted this more extreme backhand grip, I've noticed that the great majority of them fail to produce good *forehands*—simply because they don't return to the proper forehand grip in time to do so. I'm not suggesting that it is impossible to have extreme grips for both forehand and backhand. I am saying that if you're too far over on either grip, it is practically a statistical certainty that one stroke will be weaker than the other.

Interestingly, Vic Braden believes the average player is probably better off with a good backhand than a good forehand because the backhand is what is being attacked most often, especially at lower levels of play. There's a lot of truth in this—in fact, the basic baseline tactics I outlined earlier are predicated on the assumption that the backhand is usually the weaker side and the one to attack. I personally believe that most players, at any level, naturally have more confidence and strength on their forehand side, and that therefore they should start out learning the conventional forehand and backhand grips described earlier, which in fact have produced the majority of the world's really good tennis players.

So if you're trying to build a game around your forehand, as I've suggested, stick with the backhand grip described earlier, because it lets you shift to the forehand grip better. But if you have a natural flair for the backhand—if you are steady and even strong off the backhand and want to make it more offensive—then try the backhand grip that Vic teaches so effectively. Bear in mind that it will take more work for you to keep your forehand on track this way. And also, revise your tactical thinking to favor going on the attack whenever the ball comes to your backhand, and think defense when it comes to your forehand—in other words, adopt an approach just the opposite to the one I've outlined for the good forehand player.

It is natural to be better off one side than the other. It is also natural to be more comfortable and effective playing each groundstroke to certain spots in the court. Now is a good time to analyze how well you hit a short, medium, and long forehand crosscourt. If your best shot is the short forehand crosscourt, there's no sense going for a winner with a deep one in a critical situation. Analyze your crosscourt backhand the same way. Also determine how well you hit the deep forehand and backhand down the line. If you can hit either one consistently, you've got a passing shot for use when you're forced into the corner by an opponent rushing net. And if that forcing shot comes to your weaker corner, you should lob, because you know you don't have the passing shot capability from that side.

The end result of this analysis—which eventually should extend to all your auxiliary shots as well as your basic serve and ground-strokes—is that you'll know your best potential point-winning combinations. Now the problem is to get them into the match. Get used to the idea that your point-winning plays are going to take much longer to send into the game than do the bang-bang routines of top serve-and-volley players like Ashe and King, or aggressive base-line players like Connors and Chris Evert. Against decent competition, anyway, you're going to have to work to trigger the circumstances in which you can play your best shot. If your best chance to win a point outright is with a backhand volley or an overhead, then the problem is to get to net. If your best chance to approach is off a backhand near the service line, then the problem is to get that shot. You're crazy to try to come in off a deep ball to your forehand. That is not the trigger for your combination.

Alternative for a Better Backhand: The Two-Handed Shot

The near-simultaneous appearance of the powerful yet controlled two-handed backhands of Jimmy Connors and Chris Evert a few years ago gave that stroke a prestige and magnetism it never had before. We'll be seeing more and more young players in the pro ranks as well as in the schools and at the club level showing up with the two-fister. And there'd be a gap in our coverage if I didn't examine the practice of holding the racket and hitting with both hands, like a slugger in baseball.

In fact, the two-handed shot can be so good that a player would be foolish to ignore it as an alternative to the one-handed backhand —even if his one-hander is pretty good! And if you're having a problem with your present backhand, or if you're involved in helping a youngster learn the game, *definitely* try the two-handed variation.

This shot yields remarkable steadiness and ball control, and also makes it much easier for more players to produce topspin from the backhand side. The topspin backhand crosscourt shot, which has been such a rarity in tennis, is readily obtainable hitting two-handed in the correct manner. So the two-handed backhand really offers more players the chance to be as aggressive off the backhand as they can be off the forehand. It does not seem to detract from the strong forehand—as does the good one-handed backhand taught by Vic Braden, for example. It's the closest thing in tennis that I know of to having your cake and eating it too. Incidentally, my friend René Lacoste agrees with me about the long-range effect of the two-handed backhand now that it has been proved so convincingly by Connors and Evert. We both foresee a general rise in the caliber of play at the top competitive levels as more and more kids graduate into the pro ranks with their two-handers. Since these shots are difficult to come in to net against, they nullify the big serve even on a fast surface. Their presence on the circuit will force good players to be better—to be more complete in their shotmaking repertory—in order to win.

It's interesting to note that in my day the two-handed shot was considered something of a freak—not to be copied or to corrupt junior players with. Pancho Segura's two-handed forehand was the single best shot I ever played against—I ranked it even better than Budge's backhand. Segura generated frightening pace on anything hit anywhere near his forehand. Unless you managed to hit the ball three to four feet from the baseline, he would usually put it away for a winner. Segura was not alone in hitting two-handed. Vivian McGrath, an Australian Davis Cupper in the early 1930s, had a two-handed backhand and was the first notably successful world-class player to hit with two hands. Geoff Brown made a great impression with his two-handed backhand. A natural lefty, like Jimmy Conners, he hit the ball harder than anyone I ever saw—much harder than Jimmy, if you can believe it—but he couldn't do it consistently.

In any case, none of these shots were taught or mentioned in the instruction manuals of the time. That's partly because, as mentioned earlier, most youngsters didn't start seriously in the game until they were ten to twelve years old. The theory was that the

E TWO-HANDED BACKHAND HERE TO STAY

The two-handed backhand has come into fashion for two reasons: 1) children taking up the game before they're big enough to hit the backhand one-handed, and 2) such players as Jimmy Connors, Bjorn Borg and (shown here) Chris Evert rising to prominence on the pro circuits. The shot is more than a passing fashion, however. In fact, the two-handed backhand is so effective that players with established games should experiment with it if their one-handed backhands are extremely weak.

The two constants of superior play that affect conventional groundstrokes—good grips and good preparation—also determine the success of a two-handed backhand. Note in the inset view here that Chris's hands actually hold the racket in what amounts to *two* good grips—a good backhand grip with the right hand and a good *left-hander*'s forehand grip with the left hand.

Early preparation for the two-hander is vital not only because both hands must be brought together on the racket handle in time, but also to ensure that the stroke can be made with the weight moving forward onto the front foot. Very much like a good hitter in baseball, Chris steps into her two-hander to really connect.

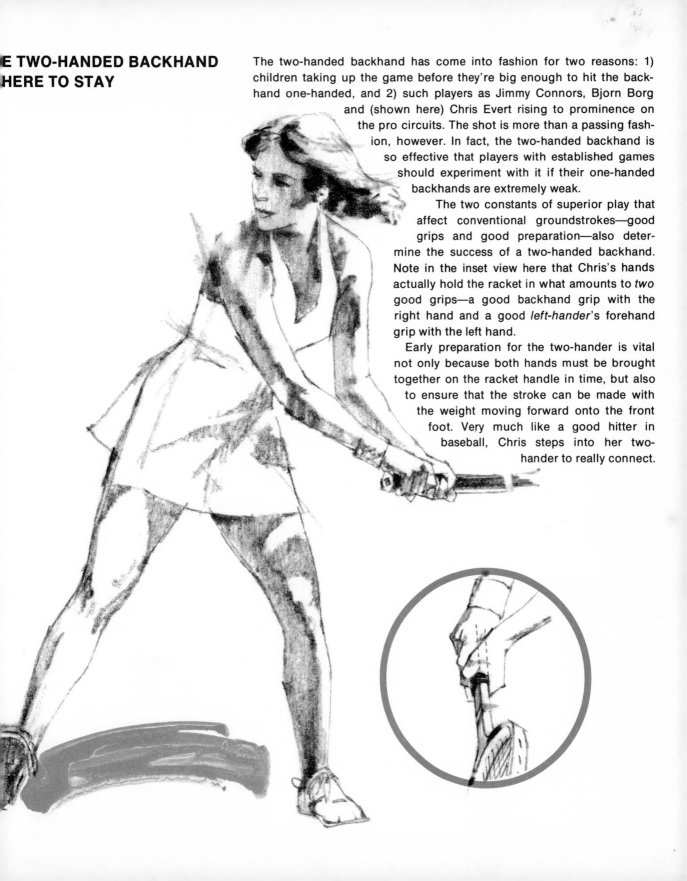

dimensions of the tennis court and the size of the equipment simply made it too hard for kids to enjoy tennis any earlier. So when they began lessons, back then, they were already big and strong enough to swing the racket with one hand.

Another hindrance to the two-hander's adoption was the widely held belief that exceptional quickness and great preparation were required to set up for the shot properly. Even today this objection is often cited, but I don't think it's valid, or rather, I think the point about readiness is exaggerated. There are simply too many players around who have ordinary skills and reflexes but who can hit the two-hander for that theory to keep players from trying the shot.

From a technical point of view, I would say that the effectiveness of the two-hander derives from sound grips, just as it does for any good stroke, from the use of the second hand to slap a little more weight into shots, and from stepping into the shot decisively with the forward foot.

The grip itself must be solid whether you hit with one hand or both hands on the racket. Some players go to the two-hander out of frustration with a weak one-handed backhand that originates in a poor grip. They'll grip with the dominant hand in exactly the same way, and find that their two-hander isn't much, either.

The position of the dominant hand in a good two-handed backhand grip is close to the position it would occupy in a one-handed grip—the telltale V's are lined up as I described earlier. In other words, for the right-hander hitting a two-handed backhand, the right or dominant hand holds the racket in the standard forehand grip *for the left-hander.*

Extra quickness in preparation makes the two-hander much more effective. The step forward with the leading foot is particularly important. It should be stressed even more than the forward step in preparation for making the one-handed backhand. More advanced players can hit good two-handers from an open stance. Cliff Drysdale produced a lethal backhand even when he had both feet facing the net, because he transferred weight into his stroke with a great hip pivot. But newcomers to the two-hander won't get results that way.

A secondary advantage in gripping correctly with both hands for the two-hander occurs up at net. Evert and Connors have both shown an ability to volley well with their two-handers. Bjorn Borg, by contrast, has had problems when he's been forced to volley quickly on his two-handed side. His more extreme forehand grip makes it impossible for him to hit anything hard on the volley unless it is a high ball, against which he can apply power with his left hand. The two-handed backhand volley of Evert and Connors is more solid and versatile because the dominant hand in each of their grips is in a better backhand grip to start with.

The two-hander may evolve out of a physical weakness or limitation, but it can develop into a strength in anyone's tennis game. It's of special interest to the growing number of kids who are starting in the game early. In fact, parents and teachers will quickly discover that the only way a six-year-old can hit a backhand is two-handed. But the shot is also relevant if you're an older player starting in the game and if you have found that you are unable to stroke firmly using only one hand. Chances are you'll be able to hit the forehand firmly, but your wrist and forearm may not be strong enough to carry you through the backhand stroking action. That's when you should experiment with placing the second hand around the racket handle to aid you during the stroke. One minor change in the grip itself: You may have to slide your thumb more around, or under, the racket handle, in order to make room for the helping hand in a good, snug, two-handed backhand grip. It's important for the helping hand to be right next to the dominant hand, so that the two hands work together. If there's a space between the two hands, your stroke will be too wristy and jerky. The repositioning of the thumb shouldn't bother you. If it was behind the handle, it was there for support, and now the helping hand will play that role.

Have a pro shop fit your racket handle with an extended grip especially made for two-handed hitters. That way you'll feel the same leather or composition material under both hands whenever you make your grip. That sensation will also help promote unity of action by the hands.

Match Your Tennis Racket to Your Game

Earlier I mentioned the importance of selecting a tennis racket with as big a handle as you can manage, to make it easier to find and keep your forehand and backhand grip positions. Now I'd like to explore the matter of equipment in more detail. A racket can be modified in a number of simple ways in order to suit your strengths and your particular playing style. If you take the time at this stage to understand these ways, you'll be more likely to find a racket that really works for you. Doing so, you can actually improve your game without changing a thing in it. Plus, you'll develop a good feeling about your racket, and that is bound to help your overall confidence and also make you play better.

As for material, I think wood rackets are superior to metal or composite rackets for most players. The wood frame is oval, so the center of the strings is not as far from the sides as it is on metal models. This means you'll hit fewer off-center shots with wood. Wood definitely gives the hard hitter and long stroker more control. Some women might get more help from the livelier 'action' in certain non-wood rackets, but many men would not be helped at all.

One advantage of the larger racket handle is that, by providing more surface area for your hand to move on, it encourages learning and keeping the correct grip positions. It also fosters more solid gripping generally. With your fingers more extended on the larger handle, you get more feel and touch. A too-small handle, by contrast, reduces the surface area of the racket you're in contact with, and sometimes even forces your fingers to overlap.

An even more important advantage of the larger racket handle is that it increases racket weight. Many players today use rackets that are too light for them. A light racket forces you to swing hard to achieve a good result. The harder you swing, the more mistakes you're going to make, and the greater the risk of fatigue or strain. Or it makes you flick at the ball, which is even worse.

A heavy racket instead encourages a cleaner, more extended stroking action. It helps you hit the ball with more spin-producing bite and pace, but with less effort. With the heavier racket you have to be sure to get the racket back quickly, or you'll be late on the hit. This is a matter of practice and within any player's reach. The benefits make it worth it.

Another advantage of the heavier racket, in wood at least, is that it will last longer. A 14-ounce racket is intrinsically sturdier and so it will stand more stringing jobs than a 13-ounce racket will.

I should point out, in all this talk about "light" and "heavy," that I am talking about a swing of three *ounces,* at most. In fact, a half ounce more or less of weight in motion at a good speed can feel "heavy" or "light"—and it can significantly affect results, as I've suggested—but the dimensions we are talking about are quite small. More precisely, most rackets sold today weigh anywhere from 13 to 15 ounces. That includes the ¾ ounce of the gut or nylon used to string them with.

Manufacturers label unstrung rackets weighing 12 to 13 ounces as "light," and, though this category is the one most in demand at tennis shops, I think the rackets are too light for players trying to develop solid, fluid nonwristy strokes.

Rackets weighing 13 to 14 ounces are generally labeled "medium" and anything over 14 ounces is labeled "heavy." Most players should pick from a medium to heavy range—from 13½ to 15 ounces— rather than in the deceptively popular lightweight range, in order to capitalize on the advantages of the heavier racket mentioned earlier.

The overall balance of a racket is a factor here. Let me explain how it works and why the ability to handle a fatter grip favors getting a racket off the shelves with optimum balance.

A U.S.-made tennis racket is 27 inches long. If you mark a spot at the midpoint on the frame—13½ inches, which is just below the head—you can analyze how it is balanced yourself. If you can balance it at that mark on some suitable object, it is "even" or "balanced." If the head of the racket drops lower than the grip end, it is heavy in the head. If the grip drops below the head, it is light in the head.

The ideal balance of a racket for any player aspiring to the type of groundstroke game that I have described is even, or slightly light in the head. Such a racket encourages a full, wrist-free stroke and followthrough.

The simplest way to get a racket that is heavy enough and that also is properly balanced is to pick out the fattest racket you can handle. If the grip size is larger, the overall weight of the racket can be greater without adversely affecting the balance. If for all that the 109 racket happens to be very light in the head—and with the variations of weight distribution inherent in wood, all rackets should be balance tested—it is easy enough to balance it. Simply attach one or more strips of ½-inch adhesive tape on the rim of the racket head until the racket is balanced, or slightly light in the head. A strip of tape placed all along the upper half of the rim will add weight and also protect the racket from scuffing.

If your hand is so small that you can't comfortably hold anything larger in the grip than 4½ inches or 4⅜ inches, then it is likely that the racket you select will be in the lightweight range that I've already tried to warn you away from. But you too can bring the racket up into at least the medium range by driving one or more thin nails into your grip with a hammer. The grip size remains the same this way, but the racket tends to become light in the head thanks to your carpentry at the grip end. This can be rectified by adding strips of tape to the head until the balance tests out properly.

So, if you are a player with long strokes and a minimum of wrist action in those strokes, the medium-to-heavy racket will make it easier for you to hit the ball hard with control.

But if you're not that type of player, it won't help you at all! In fact it may hinder you. If you are a player who has developed the short, flicky strokes which are characteristic of the one-grip method, then it is better for you to play with a lighter racket, and definitely one that is balanced light in the head. Since you don't get your hand behind shots as fully as the two-grip players do, you must depend in part on the flicking action for your power, and it's much easier to flick a racket that's light in the head.

Let me note two other controllable factors in the tennis racket and how your personal playing style may call for variations from the specifications I recommend. Those factors are *string tension* and *grip shape*.

STRING TENSION

String tension is measured in pounds—55 pounds would be medium, 60 pounds tight, and 65 pounds extra tight—strictly for the pro, or the circus strongman, or, conceivably, the good average player at 3,000 feet altitude or more, where tighter stringing is necessary to prevent the ball from trampolining off the racket.

If you're a player with long, smooth strokes, you'll get more control on all shots, including serves, with a more loosely strung racket —one in the 55 pound range. You'll carry the ball on the strings longer that way. You'll get more "bite."

If you're a flicker, though, you'll be better off with a more tightly strung racket—one in the 60 pound range. Extremely defensive players, who specialize in chops and slices, also would get more control on their shots with the more tightly strung racket.

GRIP SHAPE

A racket handle is constructed with eight sides to it, but the dimensions of the sides vary with different models. Those with relatively narrow panels on the big sides feel round, those with wider panels feel flat. When I knew I was going to have to stay back more often, as on clay, or against a first-rate receiver, I chose the flat-type handle because it helped me get my thumb into a good position for hitting backhands. That's why one-grip players generally prefer this type. It took away from my forehand, but it gave me better results on my returns and passing shots.

Play Doubles to Develop Your Volley, Lob, and Overhead

The three major auxiliary strokes in tennis are useful in varying degrees, according to the type of game you play. I'll explain the key points in the execution of each stroke, as variations on the basic strokes and the service motion, as they come up in the course of our discussion of the strategies of attack and counterattack.

The volley, a stroke played off the ball before it's had a chance to bounce, can be practiced against a machine, instructor, practice partners, or a wall. The lob and overhead must be practiced with a partner, with one player hitting lobs that the other player can smash, then reversing roles.

In my opinion, though, the best way to develop all three of these strokes is to acquaint yourself with the mechanical aspects of each, and then go out and play a lot of *doubles*.

The doubles game puts you at the net whether or not you have yet managed to develop the means for getting there in your basic

111

singles game. There you'll have the chance to volley, and to smash attempted lobs.

The doubles game also and inevitably puts you on the extreme *defensive* at times—in a way that singles play against baseliners will not, by virtue of the presence of one or both of your opponents at net while you are stuck in the backcourt. This will give you the chance to experiment with lobs.

My own singles game really did not come together until I had the chance to play a lot of aggressive doubles with Welby Van Horn back in 1939. I played the second court and was responsible for covering balls hit down the middle. I saw plenty of lobs and it cemented my overhead.

The pressure in doubles to get to net—because points can be won up there quickly—makes playing doubles valuable in three other ways for any player who's solidified his basic game.

1. It forces you to improve your first-serve percentage.

2. It introduces you to the footwork involved in rushing net, as you would try to do following at least some of your serves in doubles, and so lays some of the groundwork for a good attacking game in singles.

3. It teaches you the short crosscourt chip, a shot that prevents servers rushing in from hitting down on your return, in doubles, and can be used to counter similar attacks in singles.

Frankly I don't think enough players who are serious about their tennis are serious enough about doubles. Even some of the pros don't fully realize the opportunity that exists in doubles play for forging great singles skills.

The Approach Shot Theory

The approach shot is a groundstroke used on a short ball and followed to net, in anticipation of forcing a weak volley, or lob, and winning the point with a crosscourt volley or an overhead. It should be part of every player's repertory simply because if you've hit a shot that elicits a short ball from the opponent, you've earned the right to take advantage of it, and that goes for both aggressive and defensive type players. To hit a deep ball and get a short ball and not attack off it is a crime.

The serve or groundstroke that is so weak that you must run up into your green-light zone to hit it before it bounces a second time, amounts to an open invitation to attack. It becomes an approach shot that your opponent practically forces you to play. Weak second serves are especially vulnerable to an approach shot attack.

Against better players, you won't see as many balls reaching you in your green-light zone. But as your own stroking technique improves and you gain confidence in moving to net, you can attack off deeper shots by learning to hit balls on the rise—before they've reached the apex of their bounce.

The trajectory and speed of an opponent's shot determine how easy it will be for you to take a ball while it's still bouncing upward. It may take you a half step, or a half dozen steps, to get in position and still be able to meet the ball in your strike zone. If the shot is hard hit and low bouncing, it won't pay off to try to catch it on the rise. Your grooved swing won't operate effectively at two-foot altitudes because it's so hard to bend the knees enough to be able to hit the low ball on a level with your waist.

On the other hand, there's no point in waiting for a softly hit, high-bouncing ball to reach its apex in your red zone when you could run up and catch it on the rise in your caution zone or even your green zone. That gives your opponent all day to prepare. It makes sense to attack such a shot on its way up, to shorten the other player's reaction time and to bring you into the court.

It is much less risky to win a point off a short ball with the combination of approach shot and volley, than it is to go for an outright winner off the short ball, because your normal full stroke might send the ball into the net, or long or wide, on an attempted placement. You could go for a winner if the ball bounces higher than the net, especially if it's on your forehand side, and if your opponent has left an open corner for you to target on. That is a point-ending opportunity that you'll quickly recognize, and learn to exploit. (You would also go for a winner if you're too big and slow to chase it up to net, as I mentioned earlier.)

Fig. 1   A short ball in the GREEN-LIGHT ZONE invites player to attack.

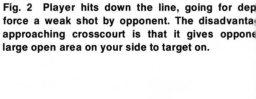

Fig. 2   Player hits down the line, going for dep force a weak shot by opponent. The disadvanta approaching crosscourt is that it gives oppone large open area on your side to target on.

Fig. 3   Attacking player moves in to volley to about 18″ to the *right* of the center line, giving opponent the low-percentage crosscourt angle, but putting himself in position to cover the most likely shots by opponent either down the line or down the middle.

Fig. 4   Player volleys opponent's down-the-line s the open corner, for what would probably be a v on a fast surface. On slow surface, volleyer mig *behind* the opponent instead.

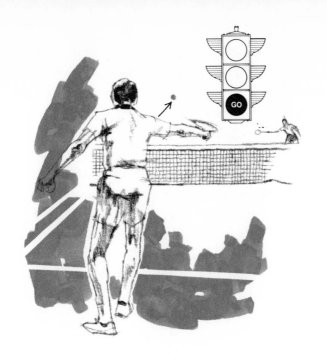

Player slices a short ball to his backhand down
~~~ ne.

Fig. 2   He moves in to a spot about 18″ to the *left* of
center line in order to cover all likely returns.

~~~KING APPROACH SHOTS WORK

~~~ g good approach shots is the only way
~~~ players can safely get up to net.

~~~ ting most approaches down the line, rather
~~~ crosscourt, permits the attacking player to
~~~ r the majority of likely returns. He can be
~~~ ed only by an opponent who has a good
~~~ oin crosscourt shot, rare especially among
~~~ hands.

~~~ nce the shot is played off a short ball, the
~~~ hand or backhand used to hit the approach
~~~ be a shorter stroke than the normal
~~~ ndstroke; otherwise there is a great risk of
~~~ g into the net or long.

~~~ ter hitting the approach, the player moves
~~~ veral steps, as shown, but not so far as to
~~~ being lobbed. Only after the opponent
~~~ committed himself to his own shot, can the
~~~ king player move all the way in for the
~~~ y.

Fig. 3   Once he sees opponent's shot, player moves
forward again to meet the ball as early as possible. If
he moved into volleying position prematurely, opponent would be able to lob him.

It would be ridiculous, though, to get a short ball, hit it, and then trot back to your baseline. For it is just as easy—easier, in fact—to shorten your stroke a bit, hit an easy slice to the opponent's weak side and with a couple of steps on the followthrough put yourself in an excellent position to intercept the next shot with a volley.

WHEN TO HIT THE APPROACH SHOT

The best time to go for an approach shot is when you get a ball that bounces at least as high as the net, near your service line and close to the center of the court. This is not to say that you can't hit an approach off balls that vary from this definition—only that it will be harder to make a go of it. If the ball bounces lower than the net, the stroke must be much more precise and controlled to clear the net and also to land with proper depth. An approach shot that produces a short ball in its turn defeats the whole purpose of the tactic and usually gives the opponent an easy chance for a passing shot.

If the ball bounces near the sideline rather than near the centerline, you may not be able to cover the open side after you've hit your approach. The shot will be even riskier off a low ball since the net is higher at the sideline, demanding of more of a lifting action in the stroke. In the one case the ball is low, in the other it is wide. Both conditions should cause the green light to switch off in your tennis brain and the caution light to come on.

WHERE TO HIT THE APPROACH SHOT

The best spot to place an approach shot is deep into the opponent's weaker side, to make it more likely that you'll get an easy ball to volley. The idea is to take the ball that comes to you in your green-light zone and hit it to put your opponent in difficulties in his red-light zone. That tilts the point firmly in your favor. A short approach shot doesn't do the job, as mentioned. A shot to the stronger side may be dangerous but that depends on how versatile the opponent's No. 1 stroke really is.

It's more important to hit your approach down the line than it is to guide it to the opponent's weaker stroke, because in doing so you will automatically move into a better position to intercept the passing shot. If you hit your approach crosscourt, you risk being passed down the line yourself because there is more court for you to cover on that side. In light of that fact, you might as well go for a winner any time you do decide to hit crosscourt off a short ball.

An approach can be played equally well with forehand or backhand. If the forehand is your strength, you'll get more chances to hit forehand approaches simply because 65 percent of the balls that come back to you will be in the center or to your forehand side. The backhand approach may be easier to hit at first because you're using your underspin or slice backhand stroke. You'll have more feel for it because you've practiced it more.

On the minus side, a lot of attempted backhand approaches come up short because the underspin tends to keep the ball short. So you have to remind yourself to get down low for it and stroke through the ball on the backhand side to obtain the depth desired.

The forehand approach is slightly more problematical. Players find that when they run up to hit a short ball with their normal forehand stroke, they send it long or, if they do go crosscourt, into the alley. If they manage to keep it in, they also find they don't get up into volleying position fast enough. You're nailed to the ground in the course of executing a full forehand, whereas you're naturally moving forward when you hit the underspin backhand.

The answer is to modify the stroke used for the forehand approach so that it is literally a mirror image of the backhand slice. In other words, hit the approach with underspin instead of topspin. Open the racket face and shorten the backswing and followthrough. In execution, it will feel almost exactly like the forehand volley stroke, only you won't be meeting the ball in front of your body, as you must do on the volley, but at the side.

Keep the racket low, too, or you'll tend to chop down on the shot. It should be as easy to slide the racket strings under the ball as it is on the backhand, and that will give the shot enough spin to keep it in, yet enough speed to make it tough for the opponent. And the forehand slice will bring you into the court as you stroke. It's easier to hit a slice forehand moving in because there's no footwork problem.

HOW TO HIT THE APPROACH SHOT

117

"SHADING" THE COURT

Upon hitting an approach shot, if you move into the court an additional two or three steps in the direction of your shot, you should find yourself on the side of the court where the opponent's shot is likely to materialize, and, if further movement is necessary, within one big stride of volleying the ball while it is still high.

If you hit a forehand slice down the line to the opponent's backhand, you'll take up a position about 18 inches to the *right* of the centerline. Why can you "shade" the court to one side in this manner with confidence? Because if your opponent is like most players, he won't have a good topspin backhand, and so will not be able to pass you decisively going crosscourt. He may be able to produce a slower-moving crosscourt shot, but from your off-center position, you can take a step to your left and still cut it off. More important, you will be in the catbird seat to catch any ball hit down the line— and that is the passing shot your opponent is most likely to try.

If you hit a backhand down the line to the opponent's forehand, the same reasoning works. Only this time move 18 inches to the *left* of the centerline. Why? Because if your opponent is on the run, as he will be if your approach was good, he won't be able to set up securely enough to come back at you crosscourt. Again, he'll have to return your approach shot down the line for an attempted passing shot, and again you'll be an extra step or two closer to cutting it off.

How to Volley

Volleying for the first time is a psychological problem for any player who's spent a lot of time in the backcourt. Going up to net is a little like the child's fearful trip into the Black Forest—you're not quite sure what you're going to find, but you have the distinct impression that your head's going to get taken off.

Some differences between volley strokes and groundstrokes originate in the simple fact that everything must be done more quickly up at net to be effective. Your ready position has to be *readier*— with your weight even more toward the toes, your racket held higher, and your eyes fixed on the moving ball. If you know the importance of this preparedness as a kind of early warning system, you may feel more comfortable at net at once, so more sure of yourself, and better disposed to adopt the necessary changes in hitting technique.

The volley is short and stiff, not long and flowing like forehands and backhands. On the backswing, the racket should be carried back no farther than the shoulder. At the finish, the racket should be no more than 4 to 6 inches beyond the point of impact. (The racket travels *4 to 6 feet* after impact on a normal groundstroke.) If your racket travels more than 9 inches after it meets the ball—that's only the width of your racket face—you are overswinging, unless the ball is an absolute setup and you're whacking it extra hard for effect.

All the great volleyers in tennis have had short punch-type strokes. All the poor volleyers have had long, drive-type strokes. *You don't have to swing to have power at the net.*

I'm a firm believer in two grips for the volley, and always changing to the right one when you have time. As we'll see later, the few situations for which you won't have time to change grips to volley often permit you to play safely but effectively in the wrong grip. But you can't change the direction of a ball hit to you at net as easily if you're in the wrong grip, or using an in-between grip for all volleys as many players do. The history of the game supports my observation that the players with the best forehand grips had the best forehand volleys—among them John Newcombe, Budge Patty, Welby Van Horn, Pancho Segura, Lew Hoad, and myself—and the players with the best backhand grips had the best backhand volleys— Budge, Gonzales, Rosewall, Tony Trabert, and Rod Laver, Laver possessing the strongest lefthanded backhand volley of all time.

If you hit your forehand volleys with a backhand grip, you won't be able really to punch the ball, and your opponent will catch up with it. If you've volleyed to the opening, especially on clay, and he catches up with it, he'll have most of the court to hit to. If you're among the vast majority of players whose strength lies on the forehand side, you're simply throwing away your best offensive shot at net.

But be realistic. If you're not able to play an attacking net game, or you just seem to lack the quickness or coordination to master the

BACKHAND

If you're a forehand player, whenever you come to net y
should be holding the racket in the forehand grip, looking
the opportunity to play your stronger shot. Changing to
backhand grip, as shown, when necessary, is a job that becom
routine in time, so that you should never have to volley with
wrong grip, at least not on first volleys.

The backhand volley is a mini-version of the slice backha
the only mechanical difference between the two strokes be
that on the volley, little or no backswing is taken. The ball is
with an open racket face, producing the underspin that provi
the necessary control over the shot.

VOLLEY KEYS

Although the volley is an attacking shot, it must be played with the CAUTION light on whenever the ball is met BELOW THE NET. You can GO for winners only when the ball is met ABOVE THE NET.

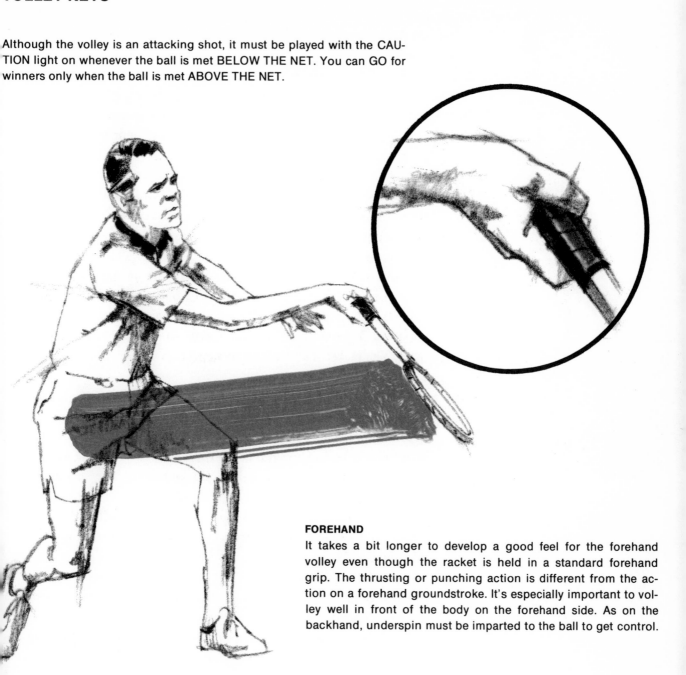

FOREHAND

It takes a bit longer to develop a good feel for the forehand volley even though the racket is held in a standard forehand grip. The thrusting or punching action is different from the action on a forehand groundstroke. It's especially important to volley well in front of the body on the forehand side. As on the backhand, underspin must be imparted to the ball to get control.

change of grips for volleys, then it makes sense to fall back on a one-grip system and to accept the fact that you'll be strong on the backhand and weak on the forehand, and generally more erratic up at net.

All volleys should be hit with underspin. A volley hit flat tends to go long. There's really no such thing as a good topspin volley, nice as that may sound. Such a shot would require a longer backswing than is possible in the time available, or highly unorthodox, not to say hazardous, wrist action.

Anyway, a ball attacked near the net carries more speed and pace than a ball in the backcourt, so to gain control of it, the racket strings must brush down on it through the interval of impact. The crisp action of the volley stroke, though ostensibly a demonstration of power, is really an exercise in control.

If the racket head is carried higher than the hitting hand at the time of impact, and the ball is met in front with a short, decisive blow, the underspin will result naturally. When the ball comes low, you must bend more, so that the racket remains above the hitting hand. The racket is at eye level at impact on volleys, rather than at waist level, as on groundstrokes.

The ball is met as much in front of the body as possible for the volley for two reasons.

The earlier you meet it, the higher you catch the ball and so the easier it will be to clear the net with your shot. Also, the quicker the ball will be back on the other side, adding to your opponent's pressed-for-time feeling.

Stepping forward to volley helps you meet the ball higher and sooner, and also gives you a better look at your angles on the other side, but there is no need to consciously transfer the weight, as there is in groundstrokes. Remember, you've already got pace on the ball by virtue of hitting it in the air near the net instead of off the bounce near the baseline. When there is time to pivot and step, you will volley with a bit more authority, but the weight transfer is nothing to be conscious of, or to strive for, on shots at net.

The backhand volley will come quickly and naturally to you because it is so similar in feeling to the underspin backhand, or slice, that you learned in developing your ground game. The forehand volley will seem unfamiliar if you are accustomed to hitting balls on the forehand side with the low-to-high stroking path that is productive of topspin. So the forehand volley will take more time to master. In the long run—and especially if you adopt an aggressive style of play—you will discover you can volley for winners more frequently off that forehand than you can off the backhand. So the extra practice required to get the hang of the forehand volley will be worth it.

Volley Tactics

Let's place the volley in the framework of our approach shot theory, see how it functions, then cover a few common problems related to its use in the heat of match play.

You've hit the approach and moved to within 12 to 15 feet of the net, shading the court to the side of the likely return. What next?

CLOSING IN

If I may refer briefly to my own playing experience again, one of the greatest assets in my game was the ability to *close in* swiftly for the kill, as soon as I saw that my serve or my approach had produced the desired reply from the opponent. In other words, it isn't always good enough to hit an approach and then wait for a floater to volley away. To keep up the attack, you often must step forward to meet the ball even earlier. I practiced this stride from the volley ready position over and over until I had it down pat. It was well worth it, because I think I got to hit more high volleys and fewer half volleys than anyone else.

The possibility of the opponent hitting a lob instead of a passing shot is really what keeps the smart player from rushing headlong into net after his approach, and why it makes this last-second stride —or lunge—sometimes necessary.

If you can get two to four steps inside the service line at the finish of your approach, and are of ordinary quickness, you'll be close enough to close in to volley, yet still far enough back to protect against that lob. If you get much closer, you'll be too vulnerable to being passed air mail. Yet if you remain planted in that volley ready position, you'll face too many low volleys and even half volleys, especially against better players.

WHERE TO VOLLEY

If the approach shot has been effective and you have closed in properly, you should have a high ball to volley and you can angle it to the open side for a winner, at least on any fast surface. When the ball comes from down the line, volley crosscourt. When it comes from crosscourt, volley down the line. Use the outside corner of the service box on the open side as your target. If you're making a short, firm volley stroke in the right grip, the ball will be almost impossible to run down, unless your opponent has the extraordinary quickness of a Raul Ramirez or, in my day, Frank Sedgman. (The quickest man I've ever seen on a tennis court was Dave Freeman, the National Junior champ in 1938 and several times national badminton champ.)

That's the theory. If for some reason you must play a low volley, the caution light should go on in your tennis brain. Instead of hitting short to the open side for a placement, volley it *deep* to the opponent's backhand, hoping for a forehand volley next time around, which you can then angle sharply crosscourt.

The caution light should also go on if you're playing an approach-and-volley combination on clay. If a crosscourt volley isn't sharply angled, the opponent may be able to chase it down. Then he'll have you in a fix because there will be a large open area on your side for him to attack down the line. If you move to cover that space, he can then hit it crosscourt anywhere for a winner.

In this case, it's better to volley the ball back down the line, playing it just as though you were hitting the approach shot—in order to get a better shot the next time. There is still a chance you will win the point on the first volley, by volleying back into the area which the opponent is leaving, because he won't be able to change direction on a slippery surface like clay as quickly as he could on cement.

124   If for some reason you must go for a placement on clay, volley it

hard down the line, or hit a drop volley. The percentage play, though, is to volley back in the direction from which the ball has come.

If you get a volley on the backhand side that is 2 to 3 feet above shoulder level, an awkward shot for even top players, you should also play it more carefully. If the opponent is wide, and you can generate any degree of power, you still might be able to knock it down the line for a winner. If he's behind his baseline, a soft angled crosscourt volley could also produce a winner. But if the ball catches you way over by the sideline, just shove it down the line as deeply as you can, get to the right spot, and take your chances. If you're on the line, go down the line.

If your volley off the backhand isn't good enough to win the point, the smart thing to do is get back into the forehand grip. More players slice and hit flat to try to pass you than hit topspin crosscourt, so in the forehand grip you'll be ready for it.

There is one occasion when you won't have time to get into the correct grip to volley.

If you are following a serve, backhand approach shot, or backhand return of serve into net, you do have time to get into your forehand grip. (If you're following a forehand approach, you're already in the right grip.) If you see that the first volley is coming to your backhand side, you still have time to change to the backhand grip. It is after playing that volley, and changing once again to the forehand grip, that the problem may arise. If the second volley also comes to your backhand—and this will usually happen only against the player with a good crosscourt backhand—the ball will be coming too fast for you to change grips again. So you'll have to volley in the wrong grip—without that thumb behind the racket handle supporting the stroke.

If the ball is above the net, just block it down the line. If you hit it firmly enough, you still may get your placement. But if the ball is below the net, immediately go on caution and simply try to keep the ball in play crosscourt, the direction in which you're likely to get more depth. A down-the-line low volley off the wrong grip would tend to land short or fade outside the line.   **125**

The Smash– Ultimate in Attack Shots

Even if your first volley lacks sting, against many opponents it still may be good enough to force a lob. The proof of your attacking game lies ultimately in your ability to handle such lobs with the overhead, or smash. If you can't volley well, you have no business hitting weak approaches. And if you can't smash, you have no business hitting mediocre volleys.

Once you're inside the service line during a point, you must be ready to drop back at a moment's notice to cover the lob. The smarter your opponent is, the more lobs you're going to encounter if you play an attacking game.

The smash requires the most athletic ability of all the strokes. It should be the last shot you attempt to master. It's modeled closely on the service motion, so you're better off waiting until you can serve with a backhand grip, good arm motion, and proper weight transfer before practicing it.

The special preparation required for fielding the lob is not a factor when you assume the serving stance. This single big difference between the shots explains why many good servers are poor smashers—they don't prepare properly.

Back up and get sideways to the net as soon as you see the lob is on its way. Keep your eye on the ball as you move back—or move forward, if the lob is extremely short—and stay on your toes. I find that it helps to remain in motion, even if you have to dance in place, in order to be able to initiate the serve-type swing at the right time. This is where the knack for timing the shot comes in. You must try to meet the ball in the same spot you would if you were tossing for the serve. If you hit it too soon, or let it get behind you, the smash tends to go long. If you let it drop too far, it tends to find the net. Most players won't generate as much power on the overhead as they do on the serve simply because the difficulty of timing the shot inhibits wrist action somewhat. And though you should transfer the weight to the front foot as you smash, you can't really get all your weight moving forward, as you can on the serve through practice.

Not as much power is needed on the smash anyway. You're not back at the baseline when you smash, and you have the whole court on the other side to target on, not merely the service box.

If you've developed a good slice serve, as I recommend, then off a straightaway lob you'll naturally place the ball in the opponent's forehand; in order to slice the smash into the backhand corner, you would have to angle your body more toward that direction in preparing.

Some top players—Arthur Ashe and Roscoe Tanner, notably—get the racket back on the shoulder, as the first step in preparing for the smash. I always preferred waiting until I could start everything together, just as on the serve, with the difference being that I took the racket directly back to a cocked position rather than swinging it down and then up.

High lobs that tend to come straight down at you are harder to time than lobs that descend on a flatter trajectory, so they should be allowed to bounce and then smashed away. Extra-deep lobs should also be played safely off the bounce—with a groundstroke or a counterlob if the opponent has rushed net on you.

Counter-attack– Shots and Strategies
PASSING SHOTS

For every attack in tennis, as in chess or football, there is an effective defense. Against the serve-and-volley player or the approach shot artist, the *chip shot*, *lob* and *passing shot* are the best defense. Baseline players in particular must master these shots if they are going to survive the onslaughts of more aggressive stylists. For use against fellow baseliners, they should also learn the *drop shot*.

The passing shot is simply a groundstroke played when an opponent comes into net against you, after a serve or an approach shot. The idea is to hit it past him, either down the line or crosscourt, before he can volley it past you. The more solid your groundstrokes, the better your passing shots will be. Pace and depth are the most important attributes in a down-the-line passing shot.

127

Until now we've argued in favor of returning all wide balls cross-court, so that the momentum of the stroking motion brings you back into the court rather than out beyond the sideline. But if an opponent has charged you at net behind a wide serve or approach, a new option presents itself—that of a down-the-line shot for an outright winner. It's often worth going for, instead of lobbing, because there's so much court area for you to hit to. Depending on your opponent's mobility at net, it may not have to be a super shot, either—just good enough to get past him and bounce in.

A passing shot that traverses the net crosscourt—virtually in front of the opponent—will necessarily land shorter. But if it is not to be intercepted, it will carry just as much pace.

Possession of a good lob strengthens passing shots. But how? A player on guard against the lob won't move as close to net, so there'll be more space on either side of him for you to exploit with a passing shot. You won't have to skim the net so often. The needle you're trying to thread will have a bigger hole.

CHIP SHOTS

The chip is a sawed-off version of the forehand or backhand—players tend to do better with it on one side or the other. The backswing is so short it might be mistaken for a volley, except that the ball is met more at the side of the body, and off the bounce.

A good chip clears the net by a foot and bounces low and within two feet of the service line—if it's on the short side of the line it's usually more effective. It makes the net-rushing opponent play a low volley or a half volley. Since he can't play for winners from below the net, it effectively disrupts his attack. It also works against the player who is late or lazy moving in to net, and against big lumbering types who do not bend their knees except in church.

The crosscourt chip can be extremely effective against the purely defensive player, too, because it lures him up into the area where he is likely to make more mistakes, and if and when he does get the ball back, it often gives you the chance to hit an approach of your own, or a placement. If you're playing doubles, you'll develop this shot eventually because it's the best way to return serve without giving the opposing net player a setup.

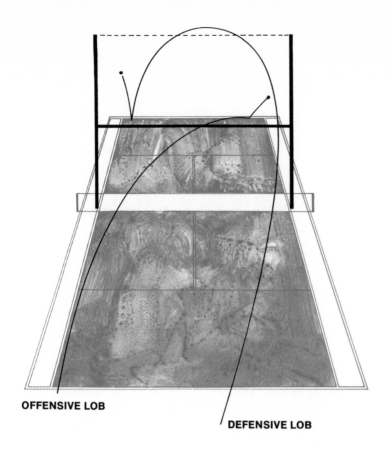

OFFENSIVE LOB

DEFENSIVE LOB

BUMP BALL EXTRA-HIGH ON LOBS

The lob is the best weapon for most players to use against net-rushing opponents with solid volleying skills. Two simple ways to become a good lobber:

1. think of 'bumping' the ball up with a compact stroke and a slightly open racket face, and

2. try to clear the top of some imaginary goalposts up at net rather than the crossbar that extra-point kickers try to clear in football. A good defensive lob should clear the net by 25 to 30′ and bounce within 6 to 8′ of the baseline.

LOBBING

The lob is a short stroke, like the volley, only the ball is *bumped* into the air, rather than punched. It's used when an opponent has moved into net against you and when you're not ready, willing, or able to pass him with a groundstroke, or challenge him with a chip.

A good lob from behind your own baseline clears the net by 30 feet and bounces somewhere within 6 to 8 feet of the opponent's baseline. Imagine football goal posts set up in place of the net posts. The defensive lob should clear the *top* of the posts. The backswing and followthrough must be kept short, as on the volley, for control. Imagine *bumping* the ball up into the air with your racket face open, and you'll get the hang of it much more quickly than off a full swing.

There are times when you might wind up for a lob, to make it appear to the opponent that you're going to hit a forehand or backhand. In this situation, strictly for advanced players, the idea is to produce a winner. The lob is not so high—it may clear the net by as little as 12 feet—just so it's out of reach of the player at net, and it lands more quickly and deeper. Imagine the football goal posts again. The offensive lob just clears the *crossbar*. It may even be hit with topspin for even greater effectiveness—but that is a low-percentage shot for all but a handful of top pros.

The basic defensive lob is quite effective enough at all levels of play. It forces the opponent away from the net and brings you back to even in the point. The longer stroke used to go for a surprise winner is crazy to try if you're in trouble, because there's greater risk of error, so you're really not fooling anybody, anyway.

Hit lobs on your forehand side with your forehand grip and on your backhand side with your backhand grip—there's *always* time to lob in the correct grip. Chances are you'll be lobbing more backhands because opponents will tend to play the bulk of their attempted forcing shots to your backhand side.

Above all, keep the stroke simple. You're just trying to punch, shove, kick, or bump the ball up into the air. It's a jab, with the racket face laid open, just like on the volley. Concentrate on *height with depth*. That combination in a shot drives most players nuts.

The drop shot can figure in both the attack and the counterattack style of play. It's seldom tried by good players on important points, because they fear their nerves will get into the act and spoil the touch required. Nevertheless it offers the chance to make a placement in the right situation. It is effective off a medium short ball when the opponent is behind his baseline. Off anything deep, it is too hard to control and usually produces a ball that goes too far and bounces too high. The drop shot is made with a volley-type stroke, the idea being to take the short ball and cut under it so that it clears the net by 8 to 15 inches and lands from 3 inches to 6 inches on the other side. The underspin on the ball prevents it from bouncing up too much. It works better on clay than on cement or fast indoor surfaces, because the underspin keeps the bounce even lower on the slower surface.

The attacking player might resort to it if the opponent is beating him with passing shots every time. Or he might use it instead of hitting an approach shot off a medium-short ball, to vary his attacking system, but he'd follow it in just as though he'd hit an approach. The baseline player would use it against another baseliner, to drive him into alien territory and perhaps force mistakes. Slow-footed opponents make good drop-shot victims.

If your opponent's attempted passing shot has pulled you very wide, or caught you in the wrong volley grip, your best bet may be to hit a *drop volley* rather than try for a placement. It is played with the same type of stroke as used for the drop shot, the racket strings cutting under the ball sharply at impact, causing the shot itself to die two or three feet over on the other side. It's easier to execute the shot for a winner if the ball coming to you is reasonably soft and on the low side. If it's too high, the ball tends to bounce up too much after you've hit it, which gives the opponent more time to get to it.

If the opponent has managed to chip a return of your serve or approach shot so short and low that it catches you around your ankles when you're two or three feet inside the service line, you're not going to be able to play a volley for anything like a winner. You'll have to play a *half volley*, hitting the ball immediately after

DROP SHOTS

EMERGENCY SHOTS

it has bounced. The key to making the shot is to bend as low as you can. The stroke itself hardly amounts to anything. The racket head is below the wrist at impact and all you're trying to do is get it back over the net and as deep as you can. The main thought on your mind should be: "Don't try to make it too good."

Part V How to Compete

In this book we have concentrated on what might be described as the basic punches in tennis, and I've tried to limit your progress in the game to those shots in the belief that they make up the ground floor of any good tennis style. No finesse shot, no shrewd game plan, no great commitment to might or endurance will ever save you in a tennis match if your basic game is spotty.

But a lot more goes into winning than hitting the ball. What about getting ready mentally and emotionally for the rigors of match play? What are the things that can give you a competitive edge in a match?

Taken together, such nontechnical or subjective concerns comprise a kind of X-factor in the formula for playing winning tennis. In the next chapter I'd like to share my feelings and observations about such things. There's no single, ready-made X to suit all players alike. But if you're to amount to anything on the court, it's safe to say that your X must amount to something substantial in your own formula.

Then there's the other guy—or gal. Tennis is more like prize-fighting than any other sport I can think of, because the opponent is always a central figure in what you do and how well you come out of it. So in the last two chapters we'll examine both the ordinary and the extraordinary tennis opponent, in the forms in which he or she most commonly appear, at the club level, and at the very top of the game as it is played today.

A top player prepares for an important match or a big tournament like Wimbledon or Forest Hills two or three months in advance. I don't mean he becomes obsessed with the match, or devotes half his waking hours to thinking about the match and practicing for it. But he does make the commitment in his head and heart that he's going to be ready to play that match or tournament as well as he can, and that sets his gears in motion.

Match Preparation

At the other levels the same kind of commitment may be desirable. Your goal for the coming summer—or for the next winter indoor season—might be to beat a certain opponent, or advance a step on the club ladder, or gain the No. 1 spot on the high school or college team. The idea is to put the challenge into your own words, and to visualize the steps needed in meeting it.

GETTING IN SHAPE

Physical condition was always just as important to me as mental condition.

I used to get in shape like a boxer. I can't imagine anything more strenuous than going fifteen rounds in a boxing match, so I copied what the prizefighters did to stay in top physical condition. I would skip rope for ten to fifteen three-minute rounds, then do a bunch of situps because I always thought firm stomach muscles helped me get down to the low ones late in a long match. For stamina I would jog thirty or forty minutes. That gave me the extra wind for going a fourth or fifth set if necessary.

After I got my game down pat, I learned to cut my practice sessions short. I spent more time keeping my body trim than I did actually hitting tennis balls. If you're a youngster, two or three hours of practice a day may be stimulating and probably important, especially if you're out to beat the world. But as you mature and your game takes shape, that much practice does more harm than good. If you're out there pushing yourself to hit short crosscourt backhands for half an hour, say, or some other special shot that you think you need, you may start practicing the shot in the wrong way. Once you're bored you can't improve anything. In fact you'll pick up bad habits.

The Australian players are justly famous for their emphasis on physical conditioning, but I think we Americans were the ones who tipped them off to its merits a long time ago. That was in 1946 when we went down to Melbourne, and handily beat the heavily favored Aussie team for the Davis Cup. During the weeks we spent there, I worked out two hours a day in a gym to keep my legs and stomach in peak form. That gave the Australians something to think about after we left with the Cup, and, in fact, not long after that, when Harry Hopman became captain, physical conditioning became a vital part of the Australian team's program.

I liked to study the competition. Many of my contemporaries felt differently about watching opponents play matches. Don Budge claimed it didn't help to watch the next opponent at all. If he played badly, you might get cocky. If he played well, you might change your own basic game, unnecessarily. I never watched a match on the same day I was to play, not because it made me nervous, but because it wore me down emotionally. Whenever you watch tennis you get involved, pulling for one player or the other, and that drains you a little for your own match.

I watched would-be opponents for tip-offs to their weaknesses.

If I noticed that a player's second serve was consistently short, I filed that fact away with the mental note that I would attack the fellow off his serve more than usual.

Does he prefer the forehand or the backhand? Players not only choose to hit their favorite shot more often, they also tend to move into position for hitting that shot even when they can't. Some players can hit certain shots better when the ball comes to them down the line than when it comes to them crosscourt. The same thing is apparent in baseball—some batters hit fast balls much better than they hit curves. If you can discover that an opponent hates to hit passing shots off a ball coming to him at an angle, you can exploit that in hitting approach shots in your own match with the guy.

Frank Kovacs would invariably pass you crosscourt if you hit a forehand approach down the line to him. But if you hit a backhand approach crosscourt, he couldn't get it past you crosscourt, and he tended to fade it into the alley when he tried to pass you down the line. So the book on Frank was to come in behind your slice backhand crosscourt.

From which side does an opponent volley better? Which direction does he tend to send his volleys? Ken Rosewall was the greatest pattern player for volleying. If you hit down the line to his backhand, he would volley it back crosscourt. Try to catch him cross-

CHECKING OUT THE OPPOSITION

court and he would volley it back with his forehand, again cross-court. Never fail.

Does he have an overhead? If you see that a player can't smash, or doesn't look too sure of himself on that shot, plan to play him differently right away. Whenever you are at the baseline in your match, and he is moving to net, and you find you don't have a nice opening for a passing shot, then up it should go, automatically.

RACKET MANIA

I had to be sure my rackets were perfect before I went into a match. Everything had to be just right—the grip, the amount of tension in the strings, the relative weight between head and handle, and the overall weight.

I must have taken after Bobby Riggs as an equipment nut. He carried seven or eight rackets with him at all times, each one tuned differently. He'd baby the one he was using, but he'd dump it for another as soon as conditions changed. He put numbers on the rackets to keep track of what each one was supposed to do. He made infinitessimal changes in head weight by adding or taking off strips of ordinary adhesive tape.

My favorite racket was so important to me that I wouldn't practice with it. I'd save it for matches.

It was through trial and error that I discovered I hit forehands better whenever I played with a racket that had a more rounded handle on it. Knowing that, I began to use a rounder grip whenever I planned to play an all-out serve-and-volley game, as I usually did on grass or on a fast indoor surface. The rounder handle also makes it easier to change grips.

I went to an extra-heavy racket against big hitters like Budge, who himself used a 16-ounce job. His shots were so heavy—they had so much pace on them—that I found myself overswinging whenever I used my normal 13¾ to 14-ounce racket. With a 15-ounce racket I could handle his power without the strain. I increased the size of my grip at the same time—from 4¾ inches to 5 inches and sometimes even 5¼ inches—to keep the weightier racket properly balanced.

138   Pancho Gonzales played many matches with rackets strung at

two different tensions. For serving he'd use the more loosely strung racket to get more speed. When he had to return, he'd run and get the tighter racket so he could block back the fast serves.

I mention this because when Pancho first burst on the scene, he didn't particularly care what he had in his hand. With his great natural talent and extraordinary will to win, all he knew was he was pretty sure he could beat you. But in time he caught racket mania too.

In my day you didn't have to worry about coordinating your tennis outfit for the TV cameras. I did my bit for the apparel revolution—I was the first player to win Wimbledon in shorts (in 1947)—but I did it in whites. For any match I made sure I brought along an extra change of socks, and until sweatlets for the wrists were invented, I always made my own, with gauze and a safety pin.

But as I've suggested, the racket was, and remains, the only heavy piece of equipment for any serious player to really worry about.

TWENTY-FOUR HOURS TO GO

If you're gearing yourself for a particular match, you eat, sleep, and drink tennis in the last day or two before the match actually is scheduled. Your goal in life becomes to make the time pass as quickly and pleasantly as possible, and slowly but surely wind up mind and body for a maximum effort.

The day before an important match, I would go out for a tune-up rather than a strenuous workout. I didn't want to take the edge off my game, or leave my best shots on the practice court. All I tried to do was to prove to myself I was still in a groove. I practiced the shots that made me feel confident, and I hit a fair number of volleys and overheads, to eliminate any uncertainty about them. It's no good practicing shots you're bad at so near a match, because it hurts confidence and affects your overall game.

For dinner I made sure I had steak. I was a steak man for years and even started eating it for breakfast. Then one morning I ordered steak and couldn't eat it. All of a sudden steak tasted so bad to me I couldn't swallow a bite.

After dinner I liked going to a movie, and then getting to bed by about 11:30 p.m. I'm assuming my next day's match would be early afternoon, say 2 p.m.

I never had trouble getting a good night's sleep until I started running the tours myself. Business and pleasure don't mix for a lot of people. I know Ken Rosewall was like that. If he had to talk to his accountant the morning of a match, you knew he'd play awful later on—totally distracted. Laver was different, though. There could be a hundred things claiming his attention in his private life and business life but he had the knack of leaving them behind him when he walked on the court.

The day of the match I'd get up around 8:30 a.m. and have a light breakfast—poached egg on toast with hot tea, something along those lines. I put a lot of salt on the egg to make sure I had enough in my system later on, especially if it was going to be hot out. If we were playing in Forest Hills weather—very muggy—I'd also take salt pills beforehand. I couldn't take salt during actual play or I'd vomit. Also I stayed away from cold drinks in a match for fear they'd constrict my stomach muscles. Warm tea with sugar was my best drink in a match.

I'd hit balls after breakfast, doing everything except belting my best serve (I didn't want to hurt my arm), and working up a good sweat.

The morning workout would loosen me up and waste more time. Also I used it to confirm that all the shots I would be counting on were still on my racket. You can't choke in a practice session. Usually you hit the ball fine. That gives you a good feeling about your readiness for a match. If you don't hit a few, you might begin to feel stale and uncertain. As with everything else in your pre-match routine, this helps keep any apprehensions you may feel under control.

It's different getting ready for a Davis Cup match, or some head-to-head match or series, than it is for a tournament. When you know exactly who you're going to play weeks and maybe even months ahead of time, you can do some mental scouting of the opposition and practice certain shots and plays accordingly.

140   If you're in a tournament every opponent may be a surprise to

you. If you're seeded No. 1 or No. 2, you know who you're supposed to play in the final and that would be the match you would key to in the course of the week. You'd play your early matches with your best game, but you'd be on automatic pilot. Your attitude should be, "My usual game must be good enough to beat these other players, or I wouldn't be seeded ahead of them. I don't care how good they look, if I play my game I'll have the edge and win."

If you do lose to an underdog, it usually means you got overconfident, or you choked—you got scared or started playing indecisively. People talk about how much pressure there is on the tournament favorite. But actually if you think about it, being seeded first creates a pressure to win, not to lose. You've got to sell yourself on that attitude or you will choke.

I'd get something in my stomach two or two and a half hours before match time, not because that food would get into my bloodstream in time to do much good, but simply to prevent the nervousness that an empty stomach causes in a person.

The last ten or fifteen minutes before you go on for your match can be crucial. Don't let anything get in the way of your limbering up. The idea is to have your arms and legs and back ready to go full speed, in that very first game, if necessary, to hit an ace, to hold serve, or to run wide for a passing shot to break the other guy's serve.

I'd loosen up no matter where we were playing. If I was scheduled for the second match in Madison Square Garden, I used the ten-minute intermission between matches to do my exercises. As soon as Segura had beaten Ken MacGregor, or Segura had lost a squeaker to Dinny Pails, I'd start jogging up and down the halls, or skipping rope, so I'd be ready for Frank Sedgman, or Riggs. I always had in the back of my mind the possibility that the very first game we played would be the most important one in the match.

Muhammad Ali always worked out fairly strenuously just before a fight, to be sure his body was oiled and ready to go at the bell. Same thing works going into a tennis match.

Going into the Match

I walked onto the court with the idea of winning whether I was the favorite or not. I always felt a surge of enthusiasm for the game and the contest coming up.

On the inside, I was nervous and apprehensive, but I didn't mind because I knew it meant I wasn't going to get cocky or overconfident out on the court. The nervousness wasn't going to keep me from being able to do the job. You're got to have genuine confidence in the mechanics of your game, or a winning attitude won't stand up to real competition.

The adrenalin started flowing just then partly because I was competitive by birth and by upbringing. My dad never had the chance to take part in sports when he was a kid, so he made sure I did. From the time I was old enough to hold a Ping-Pong paddle, he taught me to compete—fairly but fiercely—and we went through every game you can think of.

Anyway it killed me to lose. I knew how much better you felt taking a shower afterward, when you did win, and I showed up for that match at 2 p.m., or whenever, with the intention of earning the right to that good feeling.

More objectively, I realized something else about the nature of a tennis match early on. You're really committed to spending almost as much time on the court trying to lose, as you would be trying to win. So why not make the best of it? Why not try as hard as you can to win?

WARMUP

The warmup before a match is mainly of use to stay loose and relaxed, and maybe get rid of last-minute jitters.

Incidentally, if you don't feel silly doing it, whistling is a cure for shaky nerves. Former Princeton coach Mercer Beasley gave me that tip once during a match when I was getting annoyed with an opponent's stalling tactics. The idea is to get the match off your mind momentarily. You can do that by whistling, or talking to someone, or performing a couple of quick knee bends. It's a way of dissolving your anxiety, or fear of not doing well.

Wimbledon used to give players only three minutes to warm up— now they're up to four and considering six. You'd hit the ball back

142

and forth a few dozen times and then the umpire would call out, "This match is best of five sets between Mr. T. Brown and Mr. J. Kramer. Linesman ready, players ready, play. . . ." And the game would be on. (I beat Tom Brown in that particular match, the finals of 1947, in forty-seven minutes, on a day when I couldn't seem to hit anything wrong, and that Wimbledon record—along with my breaking the long-pants barrier there in the final—just may stick.)

In the U.S., players get a bit more time to warm up, and for matches at the club level, players sometimes take a leisurely fifteen or twenty minutes before getting down to business. Even with that amount of time at your disposal, you should not plan on doing much more than hitting a few of every shot you're going to need during actual play.

The biggest mistake players make during warmup is not hitting enough serves, I think. If you can hit ten or fifteen practice serves to each court, you're bound to serve more smoothly and confidently once the match begins.

If you're an offensive player, you're flirting with disaster by not getting that serve warmed up. The offensive game is built on confidence, and the keystone to confidence is the good first serve. When that starts to go, the domino theory takes over and the rest of your game folds shot by shot.

Naturally you start warming up from the backcourt. All you're trying to do is take a nice smooth cut at the ball, meet it squarely, see it go over the net and land in the court. The idea is to establish in your mind that you've got good feel today and good control over yourself. The idea is to get yourself in a happy mood.

Shortly you or your opponent would move up to net and you'd take turns hitting some volleys, again just trying to get the feel of the ball coming off your racket strings solidly. Practice your overhead while you're up at net, and make sure you see your opponent's overhead too. If he happens to miss one, it'll shake him up—like a basketball player missing a layup in warmup—and make you feel better.

READING THE OPPONENT IN WARMUP

You shouldn't draw conclusions about how well you're going to fare in the match if your knowledge of a player is based entirely on a warmup session. Especially, don't lull yourself into overconfidence if the opponent doesn't look like much. A combination of bad-looking strokes can produce many a point-winning shot.

But you can learn a few things. Generally, players practice the shots they're weak on. If you find you are hitting down the middle and your opponent keeps backing around to hit backhands, obviously he wants to get a bit of a groove in that stroke because he's afraid of it.

That theory doesn't work on the serve. Most players warm up the serve they intend to use, not the one they're weak on. So, if you don't already know from previous run-ins, you can get a little advance indication of whether you're playing a slicer or a twister.

Hit to special locations to uncover possible weaknesses. Without becoming unsportsmanlike about it, you can produce a short ball, or a junk shot, or an extra-hard one, just to see how well the other player handles it.

I should add that sometimes you run into a player who tends to warm up according to the style in which he would *like* to play tennis, and not the way in which he'll actually play. I've seen a number of lobbers and dinkers at the club level unconsciously pretend to a totally foreign style of play in warmup.

My good friend and great doubles partner for many years, Ted Schroeder, was like that. He'd warm up as though he were Budge—hitting hard, flowing groundstrokes. And even when the match began he'd keep going for those winners and not play the game he excelled in. He had a pretty good backhand and he couldn't really consistently control his forehand. His effective style was not to hit classy groundstrokes, but to shove the ball around from the backcourt, move in quick, and with his great speed and anticipation hit volleys and smashes for winners. Ted often lost the first set in a match, and could have made it easier on himself if he played his own game from the start.

144

As a rule you should elect to serve first if you win the toss—the spin of the racket—just to get that first game on the board, and let your opponent know you believe in your serve.

You might elect to receive, instead, if you happen to be a counter-attacker with a weak serve, or if for some reason you're not properly warmed up. You can use the opponent's first service game to work out the kinks in your system.

Outdoors, your choice of serve or sides may be affected by sun, wind, or even humidity.

If you win the toss, you might want to pick a side instead of electing to serve, in order to make your opponent serve his first game in the sun or in swirly winds if he happens to have an unusually high ball toss.

The sun is only a factor when it's high enough in the sky to shine in the player's eyes when he makes the toss. If you're serving from the south side of the center court at Forest Hills, in August, your problem time may be around 11 a.m. That's when the sun is in the place where you would normally toss the ball for your best serve. If you're serving from the north side, your problem time may not come until 12 to 1:00 p.m.

In windy conditions you might want to give any player with a high ball toss the chance to serve first. A few years ago I watched Pancho Gonzales, well past his prime, easily beat Arthur Ashe and Stan Smith, each firmly in his prime, in straight sets, in gusty weather in Las Vegas. Smith and Ashe toss the ball so far up that it was impossible for them to serve with great consistency in that weather. Pancho cleverly lowered his toss and settled for getting the serve in.

On hot, steamy days when I knew I was going to do a lot of sweating, I often elected to receive serve first, to the surprise of many. It had nothing to do with the position of the sun or the wind. I reasoned that I would be going to my serve after each change of sides, and that would give me the advantage of drying my hand and racket handle with a towel each time. Meanwhile my opponent would be forced to serve all of his games (except the first) immediately following the exertions of receiving my serve. If I'd

145

been making him work good and hard, the sweat would be rolling off him and he might well have problems holding the racket firmly for his own serve.

People puzzled over this tactic of mine but no one ever really figured it out until the day I was to play Bobby Falkenburg in a semifinal match in the Pacific Southwest in 1947. The morning of our match I remarked on the hot weather to a mutual friend and casually mentioned my intention to let Bobby serve if I won the toss. "But that's all he's got is his serve! Why let him go first?" I quickly explained my reasoning. The time of the match rolled around, we spun the racket, and Bobby won. At first I couldn't believe my ears: "You serve, Jack," said Bobby. But then I realized our mutual friend had spilled the beans.

WEATHER FORECAST

The sun and wind and changing weather are things to take into account before you start play, so you're mentally ready for how they may affect your performance. You must learn to recognize where and how these factors come into play, and make adaptations in your game as soon as they do.

The sun can get in the way of your overhead just as it does your serve. Expect more lobbing when it's high in the sky, at least against a smart opponent. If you can't find a ball that's been lobbed, let it bounce rather than smashing blindly. Make a mental note to give your opponent the same treatment after the next change of sides.

The wind's a bigger problem than the sun because it blows on all your shots, not just your serve and smash. It can drive you crazy if you're not prepared for it. It's particularly tough on players with long strokes and on flat hitters. In effect, the wind redesigns the court on you and you've got to aim with the new lines in mind.

One of the few matches I ever played that I recall with some reluctance took place one very windy day in Newport in 1941. My opponent was Don McNeill. He was the previous year's national champ and I was still a kid, but I had a fairly good chance in the match because Don wasn't playing that well. The wind conspired to upset my every chance to break serve, however—at least that was how I saw it at the time—and I simply stopped trying after Don had won the first two closely fought sets.

Alison Danzig came by my locker as soon as the match was over. Danzig was the top writer in the game at the time and I knew how much he thought of me from things he had written in the New York *Times*. Besides that, we were pals—he and I would split $5 bets in informal craps games that popped up along the circuit.

So I was not glad to see him.

"What went wrong out there, kid?" he inquired anxiously. "Are you all right?"

"I'm just a quitter," I said. Right away I saw his expression change from concern to incredulity. I thought he was going to cry.

"You weren't hurt or anything?" he said.

"No," I said, "I just gave up."

And at that point, I thought I was going to cry too.

I guess I never got over my dislike for the wind, but I did learn to play in it. I found it helped to shorten all my swings—on groundstrokes, volleys, and overheads. My usual anticipation and timing would be thrown off by last-second quirks in the flight and bounce of a ball in windy conditions, but from the shorter swing I could cope with the changes more easily.

I learned to hit harder when the wind was coming toward me, and softer when it was behind me. When the wind was blowing across the court I would aim differently.

All that is just common sense. The real winners in the wind are usually those who also maintain control over their serves—and who have the right mental attitude. You have to take the attitude that you're going to get the ball back any way you can, and maybe not the way you usually like to get it back, and also that you're going to lose a few points to the weather but you're not going to let it bother you. Easier said than done, but that's the idea.

FAVORITE COURTS

On fast courts like grass, cement, or certain indoor surfaces, an attacking game based on deep serves, good approaches, and well-placed volleys is the most effective style.

On slow surfaces like clay, attack tactics have to be modified or you're dead.

Stay back on your serve, keep the ball in play until you get a short ball, and when you do come in to volley, try wrong-footing

147

the opponent instead of hitting to the open corner all the time. In other words, volley back into the same area where you hit the approach shot—and from which the opponent is retreating in order to recover a good central position in the court. It'll be hard for him to change directions quickly, and if he does get to the ball, he won't do much with it.

Use the same tactic when you go for a winner off a short ball. You can get just as many winners on clay hitting behind the opponent as hitting into the open corner.

If you put a lot of stock in your serve, make a mental adjustment not to get upset when you lose it occasionally playing on clay. No serve is big enough to win all the time on slow surfaces.

Sometimes a combination of factors subtly affects play in a way that makes a certain type of player virtually unbeatable. The bounce and feel and footing of a certain court surface may suit a certain style of play, and weather conditions may add to the effectiveness. Pancho Segura had such power off his two-handed forehand that he could control the flight of shots during a hurricane if he had to. And he had great footwork and agility. If you drew him for a match on a slippery dirt court on a windy day, you didn't have a chance. He owned you.

Grass was always my favorite surface. I didn't think it was the best possible single test of tennis, but it was easy for me to be effective on it. The reason I like Wimbledon so much as a playing area was not the grass, though. It was the superb visibility afforded the players. At Wimbledon you could not lose sight of the ball in a background of advertisements or crowds, as you can in many other locales.

Intangible associations can help you play better in one place than another. I would have to pick center court at the Los Angeles Tennis Club as my favorite venue. It was in my home area and near most of my early friends and supporters and each time I went out there I felt like I was going to play great. In fact, I usually did— in seven years I never lost a match in the place.

Warming up, you try to feel at home no matter where you're playing, or what the surface is, or what it's like out.

After you reach a certain level, you might even start analyzing the court with a golfer's eye. Tennis courts can have their idiosyncrasies just as golf courses do, and knowing them can give you an edge.

Years ago the service box on the backhand court on the south side of center court at Forest Hills had a slight flaw in it that you could target on when serving. There was a slight roll or dip in the turf 2 feet inside the service line and 6 to 8 inches inside the sideline. Maybe only a seeded player—or an agronomist—would notice it. But if you could hit that slight downward pitch, especially with a flat serve, you'd produce what is known as a shooter. The ball would bounce off so low and quick that no one could possibly return it.

My favorite sweet spot was a raised seam that ran along near the centerline on the canvas surface used in my two series of indoor matches with Riggs and Gonzales. We all knew about it and aimed for it on the serve, but it happened to be right where I happened to hit my best flat serve. So I got a lot more errors out of them, using that seam, than they ever got out of me.

During the Match

I said I liked to be ready to play at 100 percent from the moment the match began. Everything I'd been doing and thinking for the past day or so was keyed to this. I'd wound up the spring and now it would uncoil.

I tried to have everything going for me. I was limbered from my exercises, relaxed from the warmup, happy with the court and the weather, confident in my basic game, and expectant that my point-winning combinations would prevail over the day's opponent. All of those things ideally were in place before I stepped up to serve or to receive on that first point.

START FAST

The worst thing you can do is start slow, or con yourself into thinking you can take your time getting into the match. The curtain is up, so you've got to perform.

You don't have to serve a lot of aces to get off to a fast start. You

149

can break a player down mentally without doing anything spectacular in the first game or two.

Against a defensive player on a clay surface, I sometimes chose to begin a match hitting steadily from the baseline, rather than trying my usual serve-and-volley game. I knew if I managed to win most of the early games that way, my opponent would start getting a desperate feeling inside. A defensive player who is being outdefensed has no place to go. He might panic, start playing shots he normally wouldn't try. If he makes a couple of mistakes, he'll get thoroughly demoralized.

It's like getting the opponent to abandon ship before he really has to. Once you have him in the lifeboat, you can sink him fast.

PLAY PERCENTAGE TENNIS

Play the game you've been practicing, not the game you'd like to play, or the game you think will impress or annihilate your opponent.

To summarize some of the things mentioned in earlier chapters, the percentages will be in your favor so long as you:

Hit the shots you know how to hit. The more often you get to use the automatic strokes that you have grooved through practice, the more effective you will be in competition. The more you invent shots to hit, the more erratic you'll be. Stick to the point-winning combinations you're familiar with. These are what give consistency to your tactical approach, whether it be attack, counterattack, or a mixture of both, or the style of keeping the ball in play with steady but not spectacular groundstrokes and a generous sprinkling of lobs.

Hit to the opponent's weakness. No tennis player is equally effective from both forehand and backhand sides. At the championship level, some players may achieve reasonable parity in their groundstrokes, but not many players. Jimmy Connors's two-hander is twice the shot of his one-hander. At the college and amateur levels, the disparity is much more obvious. The farther down you go, the bigger the gap, until when you get to the lowest level of tennis player, the forehand and backhand are equally lousy.

You must hit a certain number of balls to a player's strength because if you don't, his weak side is going to benefit from the anticipation of knowing your shot is coming there. But hit to the strength selectively, on less important points.

As a rule, whenever you have a choice—as on your own serve and on balls that come to you in the middle of the court—go to the player's weak side.

Play deep balls safely. Don't try anything fancy from a deep position, because the percentages are against you. Remember your limitations in the caution zone and particularly in your red-light zone.

Hit all wide balls crosscourt. Unless you're going for an outright winner—as you might do against an opponent rushing net—don't hit the ball down the line when you're running wide, because it will carry you into the golf course. The ball will be running away from you when the opponent hits it back and you'll never catch up with it. Hit it crosscourt and you'll arrest your motion beyond the sidelines, and the next shot by the opponent will come back in your direction.

Attack all short balls. Hit approach shots or placements off any balls that draw you into your green-light zone. It's a crime to trot back or remain in the backcourt if you have a chance to come in on a short ball.

Hit most approaches down the line. When you do attack a short ball, send it down the line on the theory that most players don't have a topspin crosscourt shot and so won't be able to pass you that way. Knowing this, you can shade the court in favor of the likely return, yet still cover the weak crosscourt shot, and volley either reply for a winner nine times out of ten. Subject to change only if your opponent can hit with controlled topspin.

WHEN TO TAKE
A CHANCE

There are times when you might as well go for broke. Say your opponent has you down 40–love on his own serve. In the course of the fourth point he forces you off the court into your red-light zone with an approach shot. Trying to shove it back safely will not really keep you in the point because he's going to be up at net to volley it to the open corner. A lob won't help because you're so wide you

151

won't be able to catch up with his smash. So why not try a forehand down the line or crosscourt in front of him? Take the offensive immediately when in such a jam. You might get the placement but, more important, you won't wear yourself out.

Such a departure from the strategy of percentage shotmaking is actually a calculated risk, not a reckless gamble. You realize you are hitting a low-percentage shot, so if it misses you won't get upset or dwell on the loss of the point. Should you make it, it could demoralize the opponent—who felt he deserved to win—and maybe even turn the game around.

I would say that you should go for a shot like this only when the balance of power is overwhelmingly in favor of the other player. The balance of power at any given moment during a point may be described as a function of your positions on the court in relation to your shotmaking options. It takes considerable playing experience to develop a sense of this balance and to be able to gauge when conditions are right for an all-or-nothing shot. I mention it to show that even when you're forced into the most defensive position imaginable, luck and circumstances can help you win the point.

TALK TO YOURSELF

I'm basically a light-hearted person, but I took match play so seriously that they called me Old Pruneface out there. It was a reflection of my great concentration.

I hardly ever talked at all once the match got going. Naturally I would discuss any technical problems that might come up, but I didn't like to. Conversations with the opponent tended to distract me. I didn't even like to talk to our team captain when I played in Davis Cup competition. I always told my captains to relax and have a good time and let me play my match.

You've got to be your own coach and captain on the tennis court, anyway, even when you happen to be playing for a team. You've got to call your own shots, and manage your skills and emotions properly, to survive the ups and downs of the typical close match. The ability to do this is just as important as is mastery of the mechanics of the game.

Talk to yourself during a match, not anyone else, and do it all the time. It helps you sustain a high level of concentration. If everything is going fine, tell yourself, "Good, let's keep playing the same game, let's not try to improve what we're doing." When you're winning and feeling good about it the tendency is to try to make extra-hard shots, to show yourself or someone else how great you are. But if you lose a couple of points in the process, it can set you back.

If you're running into problems of execution on a certain shot, talk to yourself about the fundamentals. Keep everything simple and familiar. If the serve's not going in, ask yourself, "Am I hitting it on the way up? Am I throwing it too far out in front? Should I take a little spin off the thing?" If you're mishitting your forehands or backhands, tell yourself, "Racket back quickly, hit through the waistline, shift that weight, carry the ball, bend the knees, watch the ball . . ."

Percentage tennis does not guarantee your winning *all* the points. Every shot you hit to an opponent's weak side is not going to produce a weak return. Every down-the-line approach is not going to give you a high volley to put away.

HOW TO HANDLE ERRORS

Luck or extra-good shots by opponents are inevitable. So long as you get the lion's share of the points off shots on which you have the edge, there's no reason to get rattled. And on crucial points where you play the percentage shot, all you can do is hope that the opponent won't pick that time to make his allotted one or two out of ten.

Get the opponent's good shots and your bad shots out of mind once the point is over. Keep track of unforced errors by you, not errors caused by your opponent's better play. If you hit a good approach shot and the opponent somehow blocks it past you for a winner, forget it. But if he pops back a floater and you shove it into the net, make a mental note of it—not for consideration during the remainder of the match, but for next time you practice.

If you're having trouble on your overhead, there's no sense in ignoring it—your opponent won't. One thing to try is to come in on a point that isn't important, say when you're down love–30, looking for the smash and really concentrating on making it. Force yourself to practice the shot that one time with all the self-confidence you

153

can muster, disregarding results. Making the shot may put you back on track for the overhead for the rest of the match.

ON CRUCIAL POINTS, BE THE FIRST TO VOLLEY

Take advantage of the special psychology of a break point, or certain key deuce points, by being the first one to come in to net if you can at all manage it. Especially on fast surfaces, try to be the first one to volley.

Don't try anything spectacular off your serve or your approach shot. Play that shot safely to reduce your own tension, then come in, even if your ball isn't that deep, hoping that the pressure of the moment, combined with your presence at net, will force an error.

REFUEL AT START OF SECOND SET

I mentioned how important it is to get off to a blazing start in the match. The next crucial stage in a match comes after you have won the first set. Treat the first two games of the second set as though they were the *pivotal* games of the entire match.

If you won the first set, bear down on holding your own serve and trying to break your opponent's serve in those next two games. If you try harder throughout those two games you'll get over the letdown or lull that naturally occurs at the end of a set.

Also, be ready for something new from your opponent. If he's lost the first set, he knows something's amiss. He may decide to try a different strategy on you.

What if you *lose* the first set?

If you think you're the better player, it may not be a good idea to change your strategy at all. Maybe you haven't been playing with the consistency, depth, and accuracy that you are capable of. Tennis can be a drawn-out contest as easily as it can be a blitz.

A game plan may not prevail in any obvious manner until late in the second or third set. Sometimes the worst thing you can do, if you fall behind early, is try something special to catch up quickly, especially if it's by introducing a shot or tactic you're not confident about.

IF YOU'RE WAY AHEAD IN A MATCH

Don't let up if you pull way ahead. A little complacency or laziness on your part mixed with a couple of lucky shots by an opponent can turn any match around at any point in the match, as a number of grim and surprising entries in the record book will show.

Throwing a few games to make the losing player feel better is contrary to the spirit of tennis. In fact the *worse* you beat your opponent, the better the sport you are, in my view—and the better he will feel about it. Your opponent is not going to be embarrassed if you beat him fair and square by 6–1, 6–1. He will be embarrassed, and maybe insulted, if you let up on him, or engineer a few missed shots, or give him a couple of charity calls, or start clowning around.

WHEN PACING YOURSELF PAYS OFF

There is one situation where it might be in your best interest *not* to play as hard as possible—where pacing yourself will gradually give you an extra edge over the opponent. It applies only to players who can hold their own serves, works best on cement or grass, and it pays off most dramatically in long matches.

The idea is to play all-out on your own serve—in order to hold—and on the first two or three points of the opponent's serve. Play all-out *throughout* the opponent's serve only when the score gets to be 15–30 in your favor, or 30–all—in order to try to break. But if the score gets to be in the opponent's favor, 30–love, 40–love, 30–15, or 40–15, then deliberately hit your next shot short, or lob, or go for a winner—even from a relatively deep position—in order to shorten the rally.

If this tactic is applied throughout a long match, your opponent will expend about a third more energy attempting to break your serve than you will expend attempting to break his. When the score gets to 4–all or 5–all go all-out to break serve. The extra energy you have should help you win.

Ted Schroeder and I learned this trick from my old friend and coach Cliff Roche, and Pancho Gonzales picked it up from me. It was one of the main reasons all three of us were invariably tough in a long match.

IF YOU'RE WAY BEHIND

If you're being thoroughly routed by a better player, don't resort to tactics that you know you can't properly use. Don't throw away your best stuff because you are afraid of your opponent's best stuff.

155

For instance, if the only serve you can hit halfway decently goes to the player's strong side, it's better to keep serving there—even though he is bashing it back to you—than it would be to throw in feeble serves to his weaker side.

Or, if your stock-in-trade backhand is a short slice, which your opponent delights in attacking, don't start taking a big long swing off that side as though you were Budge or Ashe, and start losing points on your own mistakes.

Go down fighting by lobbing more, hitting marginally harder on passing shots, and sticking to what you can do best in the hope that you'll get lucky on a couple of shots, or your opponent will make some errors. If you're in better shape than your opponent, especially, do anything you can to keep things going, with the hope that the other player will slow up if he gets tired.

There are ways to take chances—and you're going to have to take more chances if you're behind. But wild shotmaking is often a thinly disguised form of giving up, which really means you're taking no chances at all.

WHEN TO CHANGE YOUR GAME

If you've practiced your shots, know your strengths and recognize the circumstances that will trigger your particular point-winning combinations, that's the game you should stick to in playing anyone. Your game supersedes the opponent's game, until it becomes crystal clear that your game is not working, not necessarily because it is defective, but because it happens that your strengths bring out the strengths of the opponent.

Against Don Budge, for example, I could not serve into the backhand area, which was where I could hit my deepest serves, because Budge was overwhelmingly powerful on that side. So playing against Don, I learned to deviate from my best service areas and hit a lot of wide ones to his forehand instead, and also a number of shots directly into his body. I also gave up my usual tactic of coming in following serve, and waited for a short ball to attack.

For another example, I liked to hit to the open corners on first volleys—at least on grass—because I thought that was my best chance for making it the last volley I'd have to hit to win the point.

When you get your opponent moving from side to side, an open corner is likely to develop for you to take aim on whether with a groundstroke or a volley. That's a better theory than keeping your shots down the middle, as some tacticians urge, in order to prevent giving opponents angles to work against you. My theory's better; that is, until you're playing someone who's knocking off all your crosscourt shots for winners. Then you do hit at least a few down the middle to take away his chances for angled shots.

You have to change your best game if you're losing. But give it up as reluctantly as you might give up your citizenship—because in an almost literal sense, you're likely to feel like a man without a country without it.

I recall Frank Parker confiding in me, before a match in Cleveland against Frank Kovacs, that he had a three-stage plan for beating Kovacs. First he was going to try to outsteady him. If that didn't work, he was going to bring Kovacs in. And if that didn't work, he was going to come in to net hmself. The match began, but unfortunately for Parker, Kovacs was on a hot streak. In the first set, Parker did all the running and Kovacs won 6–love. In the second set Parker gave him drop shots and chip shots and Kovacs handled him 6–love again. In the third set Parker rushed net himself. Kovacs promptly began to pass him and eventually won 6–2.

Moral: Some days are meant for golf.

Between two experienced players of comparable skill, a little extra savvy sometimes makes all the difference.

A good player picks up an opponent's basic pattern of play very quickly. Subtly he shades the court to be able to handle that pattern. He starts leaning in the direction of the shot that he knows is likely to be produced by the opponent in a certain situation. If he knows what's coming next, it would seem that he has an edge on countering the shot even when it comes off the other player's strong side. The pattern that the opponent plays eventually can work against him.

But what if the player is being suckered? What if the other player recognizes that his pattern of play is being covered? He may

IF THE MATCH IS CLOSE

decide to continue playing in his usual pattern until a crucial point comes up. Then he'll do something different and catch the first player totally off guard.

The unexpected play on the big point was something Pancho Gonzales could do well, and it would leave opponents in shambles.

Washington Redskins' coach George Allen has done the same thing in pro football, to the season-long consternation of opposing teams. Basically a conservative football theorist, he was apt to run instead of kick on fourth and seven at his own 45 once every two years—just when you're not ready for it.

BAD CALLS

A bad line call wouldn't bother me that much in a match. If I got three bad calls from the same linesman, I had a way of getting rid of the official without being mean about it. Instead of calling the guy names, I would say, "Look, I'm embarrassed to tell you this, and I know the calls you've made are right, but I'm beginning to have a mental problem about you out here and I have the feeling I'm going to end up getting beat mainly because I'm worried about your calls and not my opponent. Would you mind letting another linesman take your place at the next changeover?" Normally it worked. The guy (or woman) would discreetly remove himself at the next pause. He wouldn't suffer public humiliation, and I wouldn't have the burden of what I thought was his poor judgment on my mind for the rest of the match.

In tennis at most levels, you have to depend on your opponent to make the calls, of course. I was raised to make calls in favor of my opponent whenever there was the shadow of a doubt about whether a certain shot was in or out. Not call a let and play the point over again, and not take the point for myself unless I was positive I deserved it. I felt I was representing my parents out there, and I wanted them to be proud of my behavior, not embarrassed or ashamed. Frankly I think this is the spirit in which tennis should be played. I notice if I'm playing social doubles with a group, people do give each other good calls, but I think it's because I'm in the group. As a rule, players tend to call the close ones in their own favor, which in my view is cheating.

Good players usually have enough sense not to try to make excuses for their bad shots. I notice that players who want to play over their heads characteristically stare at the racket strings after making a bad shot, or comment on the bad bounce they just got. A player is attacked with a good sliced backhand, so he moves in on it, not to play it carefully, as a good player would do, but to do something sensational with it—*what* he hasn't quite figured out—and tries a shot that even in more skilled hands might work only once in twenty times. So he puts it in the net and declares, "That damn ball didn't bounce!" He fails to realize the ball didn't bounce because it was hit with underspin, not because the court needs resurfacing.

Remain objective and if at all possible *placid* about what happens, in order to keep your machinery going with a minimum of friction between the moving parts—especially between the mental part and the nonmental part. A competitive temperament is not without its inner fires, not by a long shot, but it is channeled constructively. If you're recklessly explosive, and mad at yourself all the time, you'll wear yourself out quickly and play inconsistently. When you lose control over your emotions, you won't be able to suppress the desire to do something stupid, and that goes in any sport.

I've become particularly sensitive to the way top players behave on the tennis court because I've seen how their actions influence the way the game is played by kids throughout the country. That's why I've believed in a strong self-policing activity on the part of the players themselves. It seems to me there's always been more at stake than the individual's right of self-expression or the particular bad luck or real or imagined injustices of the moment.

The pros have a definite responsibility to the people who watch them, and particularly to the youngsters, who are apt to imitate anything that catches their eye and seems to be the thing to do.

As an example, two top young American players of the early 1960s, Butch Buchholz and Dennis Ralston, had still not mastered their temper problems before achieving national prominence, and for a while their outbursts got a lot of attention.

159

Next thing, young kids were throwing rackets around America's courts as though that were one of the new basic strokes in the game. It bothered me, not just because I liked Denny and Butch (who soon grew out of the problem) so much, but because it made me realize how much impact popular athletes can have, for good or for bad, on young people in these days of mass and instant communication.

GAMESMANSHIP

Loud soliloquies about your misfortune or outbursts of bad temper are easier to forgive than pure gamesmanship because they stem mainly from ruffled emotions.

Actually gamesmanship is a gray area. I think it's wrong when a player deliberately upsets the proper rhythm of play—by stalling at a change of sides, by quick-serving someone, or by taking forever to serve. In some cases it is possible to show the player is clearly in violation of the rules, for instance the one that states "play shall be continuous." In other cases it is not so easy. And in still others it may be true that nothing is amiss, except in the imagination of one of the antagonists.

I tried to tolerate my opponent's natural rhythm of play and expected him to do the same. In tennis you can't serve until your opponent is ready to receive, and you can't receive until he or she is ready to serve. It's like a pitcher and the hitter at the plate in baseball. You're stuck with each other, more or less, so you might as well respect each other's playing tempos.

I guess there are limits. I've stop-watched enough players in action to know that it takes most people only four to six seconds to serve. The special case who takes ten to fifteen seconds—or even more—to serve is going to affect your nerves and your concentration. In fact, unless you're forced together in formal competition, chances are you'll avoid playing with him.

But the vast majority of tennis players are interested in playing *the* game, not in playing *a* game. Most out-and-out gamesmen end up where they belong—hitting to a practice wall.

If talent were all you needed to win matches, then Ilie Nastase would dominate the game of tennis today as no one has since the reign of Rod Laver. If he had the disposition of a Smith or Ashe, in

160

fact, he'd have won four or five times as many important titles as he has won. For reasons of his own, stemming largely from an inability to handle bad calls or negative reactions from the crowd, Ilie has not played anywhere near his true potential. I've sat down with him and said as much.

In my own day Frank Kovacs was like that. He could do more with a tennis ball than any of us, but he never seemed to be able to win when it counted. He was one of those rare players who could hit great crosscourt shots from both forehand and backhand sides.

We never saw Frank at his best in a big tournament, where his penchant for figuring out a way to lose really showed up clearly. He got the title, "clown prince of tennis"—but not the Wimbledon title, or the Forest Hills title, or any of the other big titles that were clearly within reach of a talent as large as his.

Serious temperament problems invariably produce spotty play. The game is such that, in order to get the most mileage out of what you've learned and practiced, you've got to remain as cool and single-minded as possible, and not let anything shake you out of this mood. You can't get sad about a bad break, or mad at yourself for a bad error, for more than one point. You can't get too happy, either, if you happen to be ahead. Wait until you get in the shower to be happy.

After the Match

Shake hands with your opponent at the end of a match, win or lose, whether you like him or just can't stand him. The gesture goes along with making those close line calls in favor of the other guy, and playing your guts out to win by as much as possible, and going down fighting otherwise. After a Davis Cup match during which Ion Tiriac had practiced inordinate gamesmanship on Stan Smith, only to lose, Smith walked up to the net and told Ion, "I'm sorry, I no longer respect you, and never want to have anything to do with you." But Smith still shook hands with him.

When you lose a match there's a certain amount of sadness and disappointment to get out of your system. Gradually it will dawn on you, that if you had done one or two things a little differently, you might have won—at least if the match was close. Knowing why you lost is a comfort of sorts, and it gives you something tangible to work on in your practice sessions. It's pretty hard to straighten out a basic problem in the framework of high-level competition. All the basic problems should have been solved before you got that far. But you can refine your technique to a degree, and that's what a pro would try to do, whether it be adding another few inches' depth to lobs, or sharpening a certain crosscourt shot. So that when the pro plays that same opponent again, he'll have a little more going for him.

When you're just getting started in the game, it's important to hit with practice partners about equal to you in ability and desire. That makes it possible to focus on strokemaking, without worrying about winning points, or getting into the psychological rut of losing to more experienced players.

But after you have a degree of confidence and consistency in your basic game, challenging better players will broaden your exposure to shots. You should actually start losing more matches than you win—and welcoming the chance. If you're always winning, it means you're not trying anything new in your game. You're not diversifying and improving, and it's going to catch up with you as soon as you meet a different kind of player.

It's especially important for youngsters with long-range ambitions in the game to look for matches with better players, because that kind of competition forces you to try harder and it prevents you from forming an unrealistic confidence in your abilities and experience.

After I came home from winning the National Boys 15-and-Under Championship in 1936, Bobby Riggs took me out about twice a week all winter long and beat me 6–love every time. I could win a lot of points, but somehow I couldn't win a game. Bobby was good about it—"Keep trying," he'd say, "you'll get a game off me." And I often told him later he was just trying to soften me up psychologically for when I became bigger and better and a serious threat to him.

So try to be the weaker player in all your singles games, and the weakest of all four players in doubles. That way you'll see your best shots coming back at you all the time, and you'll learn new shots in the process.

Also, vary the opposition. It's a mistake to play exclusively with soft hitters or with hard hitters. If you get yourself grooved to one pace of play, you'll never to able to adjust to another, or to a mixed bag of shots. For the same reason, you should juggle your play and practice so you get to know what it's like to play on a variety of court surfaces.

Model yourself after good players. Youngsters especially should do this because they have an inherent ability to copy and mimic. When I was a kid I used Ellsworth Vines as my model in shaping my serve, and it was a major advance for my game. As you get older the only person you seem to be able to copy is yourself.

It's important to pattern your game after a player with orthodox strokes. Among today's top pros, Orantes, Rosewall, Newcombe, Connors, Evert, and Goolagong would make excellent models. Players with highly individualized styles, like Borg, Nastase, and Solomon, would not be good models, though you may love to watch them in action.

How to Play 10 Common Opponents

At this point I want to offer some tips on playing those opponents who may lack your range of strokemaking ability, or your ambition in the game, but who have such experience in match play that even with their limited skills they are somehow hard to beat. You'll run into all the types I'm about to describe on the courts where you play. Unless you recognize their soft spots, and know how to attack them properly, you'll be in for a lot of frustration and disappointment when you play them.

Bear in mind that it is much more important for you to build your winning combinations into an effective playing style than it is to concoct individual game plans for each opponent you face. But it would be unrealistic to expect you to suspend interest in winning individual matches as you work toward your long-range goal of possessing a complete game and an all-purpose winning strategy.

Your priorities in any match, in terms of strategy, should be:

1. Play your own game.
2. Play the game the other player doesn't like.
3. Hit the stuffing out of the ball and hope you're hot.

THE MAD BOMBER

Some players know how to hit balls at only two speeds—fast and faster. If you get into a pattern of trying to outhit them, you may well give them an opportunity to groove their hard-hit shots to the point where they are forcing you to overhit and make mistakes.

Change the pace of some of your shots to throw big hitters off their stride. They'll try to powder a floater just as they would any shot, and never realize why the ball goes long or into the net.

Alternate firm drives with soft floaters. The hard hitter thrives on speed and pace, so give him nothing balls instead. If he doesn't play your high and easy shots with great restraint, he'll make lots of unforced errors for you.

If he bombs his serves, don't get discouraged by his occasional success in acing you. Bear down on crucial points. Flat servers tend to choke at 6–all, knowing themselves that they lack the safety margin in clearing the net that would allow them to proceed more confidently.

On your own serve, bounce back from your finish so you're better prepared for a hard, deep return.

Hard hitters are usually big in size, so they don't play low shots as well, as a rule, and if they take big backswings, shots directed into the body tend to tie them up in knots. If they're slow-moving on top of all this, use drop shots, even on the return of serve when the other player stays back, to make them run like crazy.

THE POOP-BALLER

The poop-ball player may be one of the most frustrating players you'll ever face. He keeps the ball in play with high bouncing groundstrokes with no pace on them, and with lobs. If you have a serve-volley-overhead game, the pooper should not pose much of a challenge for you. You should murder him, provided you're careful. But from the baseline, with flaws of your own, you may well find that you are making a lot of mistakes off his zero balls.

The way to beat him is to poop with him part of the time, at least until you get a ball that you can hit hard. Play nice and easy until you hit a shot that puts him in a weak position and then use your Sunday punch. He can't embarrass you with any hard winning shot, so don't get anxious or impetuous.

If counter-pooping doesn't work, you better go on the attack whether you like to or not. Rush in whenever you can no matter how weak your volley is, and particularly on second serves. When you do stay back, look for chances to drop-shot. Most poop-ball players hate being at net, and the last time they made a smash was when they dropped a light bulb, so lob them a lot.

Remember, it's hard to generate speed and pace off a nothing ball. If you try to do so, you're falling into a kind of trap, and that's the poop-ball player's only real weapon.

THE CHOP SHOT ARTIST

Clubs used to be crawling with this type of player. He lacks long forehand or backhand strokes but, doing the best with what he has, produces heavily sliced backhands and chopped forehands that land short and bounce low, inviting mistakes by overzealous opponents. His shots are shorter and have more spin on them than the slicer's.

It's difficult to take a ball with excessive underspin and hit it hard, so the key to beating a chop shot artist is to take a lot off your own swing and produce deep controlled shots. You must take a lot off your own swing and once again strive for control.

Chop shot artists don't usually volley well, or produce good passing shots, so always bring them into net, or go to net yourself as soon as possible. If you normally take a step or two inside the court following serve, then don't return to the baseline, because chances are the chop shot artist will give you something of only medium depth and pace. Standing in following serve will help you take his ball a bit earlier and with more chance of doing some damage, and it will save you a couple of steps every time.

THE INVENTOR   Some players are out on the court strictly for the fun of hitting a different shot every time. They have an artistic streak, and love to improvise with each new ball that comes to them. They're gifted with above-average coordination or they wouldn't be able to experiment in the first place. The reason they don't play percentage tennis is not because they don't have the ability, but because it would be too dull for them. Also, their concentration is usually rotten.

The danger in playing against an inventor comes if you allow yourself to be discouraged or frustrated when one of his fabulous shots scores—and a small number of them will score. Accept the fact that the inventor will make a certain number of great shots in advance and they won't trouble you when they occur. If you keep your cool, your automatic game based on percentage tactics is sure to prevail over his spotty series of "oncers."

THE PAPER TIGER   Many attackers in tennis don't really have the equipment to volley and hit smashes, but they run up to net because they don't want to be attacked first. Their backcourt game is weak so they figure that they might as well run up to net, jump around, and possibly inspire a few unforced mistakes.

I've noticed that a lot of small but highly energetic players are in this category, and *if* they possess a deep spin serve that gives them time to rush up to net, they sometimes do very well.

If a player can't really volley and hit overheads, you must call his bluff. Feed him low volleys and lobs rather than going for dramatic passing shots.

But the best way to beat these jumping-jacks is to beat them to the net. Go in on everything you can, especially your serves. If they don't have a deep serve, stand in close so that you can hit more returns at their feet and attack more easily off second serves.

When they are at the baseline, beware of setting them up to hit balls on the run all the time, because that may be their specialty if they're extra fast. Attack them down the middle, instead.

THE CENTRE COURT MENTALITY

Occasionally a player will come on so intensely competitive—as though he were on Wimbledon Centre Court—that he'll win matches on attitude alone. This is the determined, fierce type of competitor who doesn't know what it means to play a social game of tennis. You may be better than he is, but he's likely to beat you if you don't take him seriously.

In tennis, the desire and ability to compete can often overcome lack of shotmaking skills, so don't underestimate the no-shot trier when you run into him. He's usually very fit, and he gets tougher in long matches. Take him seriously or you may regret it.

QUICK HANDS

Some players are gifted with fast reflexes. They may not be able to do much anywhere else on the court, but when they're at net they produce wonders.

That can be demoralizing if you're the more complete player, so concentrate on keeping all serves and ground shots as deep as possible, to keep him away from net in the first place. Your best weapon is to get to net first.

When the opponent does get to net, play your passing shots *conservatively* because he probably doesn't possess a putaway volley. A few soft, low, passing shots will reveal if this is the case. If in fact he's not a firm, secure volleyer, you'll get lots of good chances to pass him on your second shot, and that's the one you should wait for.

THE ONE-GRIP MAN

Players who hold the racket in a Continental or backhand-type grip for all their shots may be vulnerable to two types of attack.

In rallys from the baseline, they can be tricked by hitting a sequence of three or four shots to their backhand, moving them gradually to one side of the court, so that they are nice and grooved from that side. Then slip a fast one to their forehand side. It's important to hit that with extra pace, so they don't have quite so much time to prepare. The idea is to get them into hitting with a grip that feels slightly wrong to them, and force a mistake.

One-grip players usually have better backhands than forehands because they have to use lots of wrist action on the forehand side. Exploit this by forcing them to volley and hit passing shots with the

167

THE ONE-SHOT SPECIALIST

forehand. You'll find they make many more errors off that side than they do off the backhand.

A lot of players grow up hitting just one stroke—usually it's the forehand to the detriment of the backhand. At first glance it might seem logical to attack the weak side—but in many cases that would be wrong. Any player with years of specialization in one stroke has built up a series of court movements and other compensations that tend to make it hard for other players to get at his weakness.

Against such players, it is often necessary to hit your serve and even your first shot off the ground to his forehand in order to open up the weakness for a more penetrating attack. Say this opponent is receiving serve, shading the court to protect his second-rate backhand. To serve into that backhand may take such precision on your part that you risk faulting. In this case it's better to serve wide to his forehand and stay back, anticipating a strong return. Then hit to his forehand again, only wider so that you begin to expose his backhand flank. On the next shot you may be able finally to attack the weak side.

If the player's No. 1 shot is his backhand, serve wide to his forehand to get the weak return. Then hit to the backhand side, even though that's his strength, to make him run. Chances are the next shot will come back crosscourt. If it's weak, you can hit it hard to the open forehand corner again, possibly for a placement.

No player with an extra-strong shot is going to be easy to beat, however. He knows what he's got and he's going to do everything he can to use it. Be prepared to battle long and patiently against him.

THE SOUTHPAW

I'm no expert on playing left-handers, I'm afraid. During what I consider my hottest playing streak on the circuit in 1946 and 1947, I lost only two matches of consequence, and they were to lefties— one to Gayle Kellogg, a real unknown in the first tournament I played after the war, and the other to Jar Drobny at Wimbledon.

My main problem playing left-handers was that my attacking game constantly played into their strength—solid, left-handed, topspin forehands. Since I didn't play that many left-handers—they weren't as common in tennis as they are nowadays—I never bothered to make the big adjustments in my game that would have been required.

And a tough lefty does require adjusting to.

On service, always put the ball to their normally weaker backhand. If that side is considerably weaker than the forehand, try to keep the ball in that area until you can make an approach shot—also to the backhand—and then move in for a possible winning volley.

If you are forced to play to a left-hander's forehand, you'll find that they prefer to hit the majority of their shots crosscourt; knowing this, you'll be better prepared to handle them.

Returning a left-hander's serve seems to be the biggest problem right-handers have because it disrupts a right-hander's normally stronger forehand. You'll discover right away that if you attempt to move around the serve to hit a forehand you'll make errors you never made before. That's because the different spin on the serve throws the ball more to your right, way into the alley in the first court. So when you do play your forehand off of a left-handed serve, aim for the center of the court on the return. You'll find it will drift along close to the sideline, but still stay in.

Actually, it's often better to get the ball on your backhand because the spin won't disrupt your normal backhand slice at all.

Basically, the best way to play good left-handers is to treat the forehand half of their court as out of bounds. Keep it going constantly to their backhand side.

Finally, I'd like to propose a practical exercise to really broaden your tactical imagination. The exercise is to figure out the best ways to play top players in the world today. I think by analyzing the varied and various styles of these stars, and trying to come up with possible winning strategies to use against them, we may be able to shed even more light on the complexities of match play.

How to Play 10 Uncommon Opponents

I also think it will help you in developing a sense of how to play the many opponents you will face whose weaknesses are not so vulnerable as those described in the previous chapter.

Here are ten players I've picked off the top of the computerized world rankings of the Association of Tennis Professionals:

Jimmy Connors	Arthur Ashe
Guillermo Vilas	Tony Roche
Ken Rosewall	Ilie Nastase
John Newcomb	Harold Solomon
Bjorn Borg	Rod Laver

Want to play them?

JIMMY CONNORS

Jimmy is basically a groundstroke player—more like Don Budge than anyone I've seen in years—who hits with such speed and control that it's practically impossible to attack him constantly off your serve unless you have remarkable control yourself.

The money serve against him is a heavy slice, wide in the first court and down the middle in the second court. In other words, make him reach on the side of his two-handed backhand. If he has to reach too far, his two-hander won't be quite as potent. In the first court it will pull him off court and open up some space for you to attack with a volley.

If you have to play a second serve to Connors, I think it would be wise to slice the ball into his body if you can. If you got it into his forehand, he might miss a few. The shot would be coming into him in the same troublesome way a left-hander's good serve comes into a right-hander's forehand. If you got the serve into his two-handed backhand, it would be all right, too, because I don't think he's quite as good moving *around* to hit his two-hander as he is moving *in toward* the ball.

Moving in to volley following a good slice serve in either court, keep in mind that you want to hit to open court. That means you're volleying to his forehand. Against most lefties that would be the low-percentage shot, but Connors's two-handed backhand is so

170

good that you would be crazy to give it to him to hit unless you absolutely had to. You could almost count on him hitting it past you crosscourt with it. His forehand is dangerous too, but I think he'd miss from that side more often.

You don't have to worry about Jimmy coming in on his own serve a lot because he's not that good a volleyer—not yet, anyway. I wouldn't go for outright winners off your return, though. Instead, I'd chip him short. He has a longish volley stroke, relatively weak in relation to the rest of his game, and I'd encourage him to make mistakes with it.

Present thinking on Connors seems to dictate coming in on him all the time, but I wonder if a more delayed attack style might not be more effective. I'd try it. I'd also lob Jimmy an awful lot. Part of his game is built around his tremendous speed and reflexes. If you can wear him down just a little, he might start missing some groundstrokes. He'd certainly be weaker at net.

But it depends on your serve. In fact, I'll say flat out that if you don't have a whopper of a serve, Connors will knock you right off the court.

GUILLERMO VILAS

You should play Vilas according to the surface you're on. At this early point in his career—he's as young as Connors and may be a long way from rounding out his game—he is not really that comfortable up at net. So I would serve and come in on him on grass and on all fast indoor surfaces. I would serve mostly to his backhand even though his topspin backhand is his best shot—very similar to Rod Laver's. But against a good serve he won't be able to uncork it—he'll have to slice or chop the ball back. Then make your first volley into his forehand. Don't volley *wide* to his forehand because when he runs for a forehand he can generate an awful lot of topspin off it, and he'll pass you.

Attack Vilas on his own serve by chipping to force low volleys which seem to be his big weakness at net. His overhead appears solid so I wouldn't lob him unless I had to.

Meeting Vilas on clay is more problematical. He can attack you from the baseline with topspin shots from either side and he's also

171

a good drop-shotter. I would take a lot of pace off the ball against him on clay. He swings so hard that you really are helping him when you hit hard, too. I'm betting he'll make more mistakes off nothing balls.

No matter what surface you play him on, be wary of letting him hit his big topspin backhand on important points. In pressure situations good players always hit their best shots better.

KEN ROSEWALL

I got trounced by Rosewall on one of our tours, 22 matches to 4. I won a set from him in about a dozen of the matches I lost. In four other losses I had had him at match point. So it wasn't quite as bad as the overall score makes it seem, but plainly Ken could handle me. He was twenty-two, awfully quick, and already fully possessed of that fantastic natural backhand of his, which he could hit from any position. I was thirty-six or thirty-seven and not in the best of shape, and he wore me down with lobs.

If we had met when we were both in our playing primes, Rosewall would still have been a tough match for me because I was a forehand player and he was a backhand player. All my strengths went into his strengths. I think I might have had an edge because my serve was much more effective than his. Ken's serve, which I helped him to bolster a bit while we were on that tour together, was weak as a kitten compared to the rest of his game.

The right way to play him? Serve and come in to prevent him from using that backhand on approach shots. He could take any short-to-medium-deep ball and slice it back to within ten inches of your baseline, time and time again. From that depth it's almost impossible to pass him.

As against any player with a strong defensive game, make sure you serve with a broad mixture of shots to Rosewall, including a few fast ones to his backhand even though he always seems to be ready on that side. And keep the serve deep because if you come in on any short serve he will chop you up.

I saw Tony Trabert use an effective tactic against Rosewall. He would serve floaters to Ken's forehand and come in on them. Rosewall couldn't hit the forehand down the line, as a rule, and he made mistakes off the off-pace serve when he tried to hit it crosscourt.

Rosewall has a great overhead for a small man, and his training program has kept him in top shape. I thought his reaching the final at both Wimbledon and Forest Hills in 1974, at age forty, was one of the most amazing feats I'd ever seen in tennis.

So make sure you're in shape when you play him no matter how much younger you may be.

JOHN NEWCOMBE

At last we come to a dedicated net-rusher of the old serve-and-volley school. Indeed, it's interesting that the bulk of the players on this top-ten list happen to be strong groundstroke players. Only Newcombe and Ashe are really big servers. It shows how the game is changing.

Newcombe is not just a big server, however. In fact I would classify him as the most complete player of all the players mentioned here. He's the one who comes closest to the all-purpose, all-court style I think young players and other newcomers to the sport should aspire to.

Newcombe has three or four great strengths and no glaring weakness—though for a top-notch player his backhand might be called pretty average. He's got a hard first serve and one of the best second serves we've seen on the circuit in a long time. He's got one of the best overheads we'll ever see. Plus a fine forehand return of serve and a sensational volley off both sides.

To play him at his peak, you've got to keep the ball on his backhand side 90 percent of the time, or you're dead. Make him hit backhands from the baseline and also at net. I would lob him, too—not with the idea of winning many points, but to force him a step or two farther back from net, so you at least have a chance to put a few passing shots by him.

Newcombe is strong as an ox so, at least until injuries began to plague him, has been able to hold up through the big five-set tournaments like Wimbledon and Forest Hills better than most. Also he's blessed with what might be called a center-court nervous system. He doesn't seem to get flighty or tight on the big occasion.

I thought Borg might be vulnerable on fast surfaces like grass until I watched him during Wimbledon in 1976. On his way to winning

BJORN BORG

173

that title, he made two adjustments in particular that impressed me with his adaptability and his dangerousness on all surfaces.

He flattened out his stroking motion somewhat, reducing that extreme vertical lift of his, and so got better depth off the ground. And he improved his serve when he needed to, as he did against Roscoe Tanner. In that match he hit a lot of great wide slices, just the thing against Roscoe, and his serve was never really in jeopardy. He outserved the server.

In any event, Borg has shown that he can be a much bigger threat on serve than any other groundstroke player right now. The serve may get even better as he gets a bit older and heavier.

On clay Borg is formidable. He anticipates well, makes shots quickly when he wants to, and he has such wrist control that he can impart heavy topspin on balls from either side. No one hits with more topspin. No one mishits more balls, either—when his timing isn't just right you'll hear the ball come off the gut and catch the rim of the frame on the way. He strings his racket at 80 pounds tension. If the average player tried to use Borg's racket his arm would fall off.

Borg's topspin haymakers sometimes produce short balls—balls that land near the service line. That's one thing I'd watch for in playing him on clay. I might try to bring him to net with drop shots, too, so I could attack his volley, particularly on his backhand, which is hit with such a poor grip that he can only hit cautiously or drop-shot, especially on low balls. I wouldn't expect any mistakes off his overhead, though.

Borg is the sort of player you have to worry about until you are safely in the locker room with the trophy. Like Schroeder and Falkenburg in my day, he seems to have such competitive zeal, and such a wonderful feel for the dynamics of match play, that when it gets to be a real horse race out on the court, he's usually the one who ends up winning, and not the player with the classic strokes.

Incidentally, the shorter matches and the use of tie-breakers on today's circuit tend to favor the player with the mechanical ability a bit more, by giving the guts-and-gritted-teeth competitors less time to work their spell.

Borg is almost four years younger than Connors or Vilas. I don't think I've seen anyone this good this young since Lew Hoad or Ken Rosewall first came on the scene.

The fact that he developed such a winning game so quickly in his native Sweden, where the opportunities for tennis are minuscule compared to those available to youngsters in America and Australia, say, has to rank as one of the great success stories in modern sport.

ARTHUR ASHE

As with playing Rosewall, I would be hitting from my strength to the opponent's strength, so I might have some problems playing Ashe. Arthur can do almost anything with a deep ball to his backhand side. He can hit it flat down the line or crosscourt with topspin. Or he can slice it deep, or drop-shot it or—as he seems to have finally discovered in beating Connors in the 1975 Wimbledon final —he can lob.

It makes sense to attack his forehand, therefore, and I would do that on the serve a lot. He takes a big belt at the ball from that side but he makes mistakes on it.

When he's serving, he'll usually come to net except on clay. He has a great first serve but if you can chip it back low you might give him trouble. That's because he often plays for a little better shot off his volleys, especially his forehand volleys, than he really should, especially on important points. If a player has this disposition for risk at net, leave it up to him to make the good shots rather than trying low-percentage shots yourself. He's going to try to make just as good a play off your tough shot as he would off your easy shot, so let him make mistakes and cut down on your own.

Ashe's winning percentage in big matches is not as good as it could have been, for someone with his ability. I think that's partly because he has so many outside interests. In any case, if I were in a big match with him, I would make it a point to try to stay with him for as long as I could, hoping that he would begin to overplay shots and start beating himself.

Actually, Arthur is one of the few guys I would not feel badly losing to, which simply shows how much I have admired his own great sportsmanlike attitude in and out of tennis.

175

TONY ROCHE

Roche is a left-handed serve-and-volley player. On clay he's manageable but on grass he moves up into the top ranks. He has a complete game and that's why he plays a lot of long matches. No one gets rid of him fast.

Tony's weakness is not that famous elbow of his, I think, but his backhand. If he's sure of himself, his backhand can be tremendously dangerous. But if he misses a couple he may lose confidence in it. My strategy against him on any surface would be to try to break down the backhand.

Roche has a good serve, a great volley, and a fine lob. He's always tough to beat on a fast surface. I think the Wimbledon bookmakers had him pegged all wrong for the 1975 tournament—33 to 1 in the singles. He eventually lost in five sets to Ashe in the semis, but in my view he was just about the favorite to win that year, what with Newcombe absent and Smith in his slump.

If he had won, the bookies would have lost a bundle.

ILIE NASTASE

Shot for shot Nastase probably has the most ability of anyone playing competitive tennis today. He also has a great ability to anticipate shots and to move on the court. He's quick and he's strong. The only thing he lacks is the ability to control the little things on the court, and that has been his undoing.

Many of his much-publicized difficulties with officials stemmed originally from difficulties with the crowd. Nastase is so good that sometimes he can make his opponent seem almost ridiculous. He may not do this deliberately, but unfortunately his gestures and manner sometimes convey to the crowd that he knows how good he is, and it annoys them. He has a way of bringing out the underdog complex in the most passive of crowds. Once the crowd starts rooting for his opponent, he gets mad at the crowd. He thinks he's the one they ought to cheer and love. What next? Arguments about line calls and other technicalities, near defaults.

I think the lesson for ordinary players in all this is to recognize and respect the disruptive effect that "the little things" can have on your concentration and play. Pancho Gonzales got mad in matches, but he managed to channel his fury into his game. If you can't isolate yourself from distractions—and many volatile personalities can not—then try to convert your feelings about them into some kind of constructive playing pattern.

From a tactical point of view, I would work on Nastase's backhand and avoid his forehand altogether, because he tends to be able to hit it to exactly the spot you think is safe.

Nastase's second serve isn't that good, so I would stand in close to attack him on that when I got the chance. When he came to net I wouldn't panic, either, or try to do too much with my own shot, because he usually has to hit three or four volleys before he can really put the ball away.

Solomon is a feisty competitor and a real problem on clay if you're not patient enough to wait until you can use your best shot against him. He is similar in playing style to Borg, except that his serve can be pushed around and Borg's can't. That means when a good attacking player faces Solomon, he's in a position to get the first ball to really hit on most points, not only on his own serve, but on Harold's, too. That's a tremendous advantage, and on grass it's even more of an edge.

Still, the attacking player must tell himself before the match to plan to take more time and to hit many more balls than he's used to, or he could be trapped into making all the mistakes out there. Once you realize an opponent has no guaranteed point-winning combination he can spring on you, you can relax and pick your shots for going on the attack.

Solomon is the best example today of the type of player who never misses a ball unless he is really forced to miss. He probably gets more good results from his limited strokes and natural ability than any other player on the circuit. He's a mighty competitor and must be admired for it.

Most champions have won by finding a system to make the other player make the mistakes. Not Laver. His game plan was: hit the ball hard and, if that doesn't work, hit it harder until the feel and the confidence returns and the match is won. He hated to hit the

177

ball in an ordinary fashion, especially on slower surfaces. He would go for depth, and then more depth. If he was getting a good angle on a certain shot, he would go for a sharper angle next time. He hit more placements to win matches than any of his contemporaries. He was similar in his ultra-aggressive style to Ellsworth Vines, Don Budge, Frank Kovacs, and Jimmy Connors. To play any of them, you had to do something special, because your normal game wasn't going to get you anywhere.

Laver would chew you up unless you served very well, first of all. On grass I would try to serve wide to him a lot. That would keep him from getting set in time to hit topspin off his backhand.

When Laver lost matches, it was usually because of serving too many double-faults, oddly enough. When his serve was off, it would also affect other parts of his game. Aside from wishing for one of those days when facing his serve, I would also attack Rod's forehand volley whenever he came to net. Normally you try to find a player's backhand up at net, but Laver was so good on that side he could volley it down the line to within a foot of the baseline, every time you did so. His forehand volley tended to produce mistakes, though —especially if he had hit a backhand on the previous shot.

No player in the last couple of decades has gotten more respect from fellow players than Rod, not only for his super abilities but for his sportsmanship and fairness. The balance he managed to strike between sporting attitude and competitive desire is well worth emulating by anyone starting in the game.